Asian Salads

72 Inspired Recipes from Vietnam, China, Korea, Thailand and India

MAKI WATANABE

TUTTLE Publishing

Tokyo | Rutland, Vermont | Singapore

Contents

Chapter 3
SEAFOOD SALADS

Chapter 4
SALADS WITH MEAT AND CHICKEN

Chapter 5
SALADS WITH FRITTERS, SPRING ROLLS AND OTHER FRIED SNACKS

Chapter 6
STIR-FRIED SALADS AND VEGETABLES

MY LIFE-LONG PASSION FOR ASIAN SALADS

Whenever I visit Vietnam, Thailand, China, India and other countries around Asia, I am always surprised at the abundance of vegetable dishes. I find dishes that are full of herbs, or encounter vegetables that I have never eaten before. Sometimes the vegetables are briefly boiled and then dressed, quickly stir-fried, or speedily deep-fried; each cooking method is so simple, yet they yield so many variations. I am convinced that one of the reasons I'm so enamored with various Asian cuisines is because they allow me to eat so many vegetables!

In this book, I will introduce you to salads from various Asian countries. As I put these recipes to paper and reminisce about all of the Asian vegetable dishes I have eaten, I am once again reminded that Asia is truly a vegetable utopia! With that as my inspiration, I developed this collection of recipes using the strongly flavored vegetables I've encountered that I have come to love, as well as more familiar vegetables from my home country of Japan and other ingredients that are used in the Asian countries I cover in this book, along with the seasonings and cooking methods typically used there.

From simple vegetable-only recipes that are perfect as side dishes or for eating with an alcoholic beverage, to filling main dish salads containing meat or fish, all the recipes in this book are very easy to make. On Page 15, I give recipes for some versatile dressings that effortlessly bring the flavors of each country's cuisine to any salad. I hope you'll use them to enjoy the tastes of these countries as part of your everyday meals.

Regardless of your status as a world traveler, this book will help you explore and enjoy the tastes and aromas from across Asia.

—Maki Watanabe

This book includes salads from these countries

CHINA

Official Name: People's Republic of China
Capital City: Beijing
Currency: Yuan (CNY)
Time Difference: Beijing (CST) is 13 hours
ahead of New York, NY (EST)

INDIA

Official Name: India
Capital City: New Delhi
Currency: Indian Rupee (INR)
Time Difference: 10½ hours ahead of
New York, NY (EST)

VIETNAM

Official Name: Socialist Republic of Vietnam
Capital City: Hanoi
Currency: Vietnamese Dong (VND)
Time Difference: 12 hours ahead of
New York, NY (EST)

THAILAND

Official Name: Kingdom of Thailand
Capital City: Bangkok
Currency: Thai Baht (THB)
Time Difference: 12 hours ahead of
New York, NY (EST)

KOREA

Official Name: Republic of Korea
Capital City: Seoul
Currency: Korean Won (KRW)
Time Difference: 14 hours ahead of
New York, NY (EST)

Asian Seasonings and Pantry Items

Here are some of the seasonings, spices and pantry items from various Asian cuisines that are used in this book. You can buy these ingredients at Asian grocery stores, stores dedicated to the cuisine of each country and online. They will add an authentic taste to your dishes.

Southeast Asian seasonings

Vietnamese *nuoc mam* (pictured left) and Thai *nam pla* (middle) are fish sauces. They are made with salt-cured and fermented fish, and are integral to Southeast Asian cuisine. The Japanese fish sauce *shottsuru* has a similar taste. Coconut milk, pictured right, is made by adding water to shredded coconut and straining the mixture. It has a subtle sweetness and is used mostly in stewed dishes.

Chinese seasonings

Shaoxing wine (far left) is brewed from short-grain or mochi rice. It has a complex flavor with bittersweet notes. In this book I have used one that has been aged for 12 years. Kojun vinegar (second from left) is a type of black vinegar from Jiangsu province in China; this one is aged 8 years. You can substitute another black vinegar in any recipe that calls for it. Oyster sauce (center) is a rich sauce made with oysters. Sesame oil (second from right) adds a wonderful nutty aroma to dishes. On the far right is another delicious black vinegar from Taiwan.

Chinese pantry ingredients

Dried tofu (left) is made by drying and thinly slicing tofu. It is also sold labeled as shredded tofu or dried bean curd. It has a unique light taste and chewy texture, and is often seen in dishes dressed with coriander at Chinese restaurants. To the right is century egg or *pidan* from China. This is made by preserving duck eggs in salt, rice hulls and other ingredients for several weeks to several months. The eggs have a very distinctive flavor.

Various dried spices

Curry powder (top right) is a mixture of several spices. Cumin powder (bottom left) has a subtle bitterness and a strong fragrance. Whole cumin seeds are also used in this book. Chili powder (second from left) is a mixture of powdered chili pepper and other spices. Turmeric (second from right) is known for its unique, vivid yellow color. *Garam masala* (bottom right) is a mixture of various spices that is often used to add flavor and fragrance.

Hot and spicy ingredients

Coarsely ground dried red chili pepper (top left) is commonly used in Korean cuisine. Next to it are whole dried chili peppers, also called "dragon's nails" in Japan. On the upper right is *gochujang*, a Korean fermented red chili paste with a spicy yet sweet taste. On the bottom are fresh chili peppers; the red ones are simply ripe green chili peppers. There are many varieties of chili peppers, with varying degrees of heat.

For adding fragrance and umami

Five spice powder (in the jar) is a mixture of spices including cinnamon, cloves and star anise. Dried shrimp (upper left) are packed with shrimp flavor and umami. *Douchi* (top right) are fermented black soy beans from China; they are quite salty and very flavorful. Szechuan or Sichuan pepper (bottom right), has a tongue-numbing bite and is very fragrant. At the bottom is star anise. All are used commonly in Asian cuisine.

Basic Asian Cooking Terms

This page lists the words in each language from various Asian cuisines for cooking methods such as mix, fry, pickle and stir-fry, as well as other terms related to cooking from each country. Some may be difficult to pronounce, but just being able to recognize some of the vocabulary will make these cuisines feel more familiar.

Toss	Deep-fry	Pickle	Stir-fry

Toss

Vietnam
Trộn
Example: gỏi trộn →
mixed salad

Thailand
ยำ (yum)
Example: ยำตะไคร้
(yum takrai) → lemongrass
salad

China
拌 (ban)
Example: 涼拌粉絲 (liang ban
fen-si)→ glass noodle salad

Korea
무치다 (muchida)
Example: 오이무침 (oi-mu-
chim) → spicy cucumber

Deep-fry

Vietnam
Chiên
Example: chuối chiên
→ fried banana

Thailand
ทอด (tod)
Example: ทอดมันปลา
(tod mun pla) → deep-fried
fish cakes

China
炸 (zha)
Example: 炸鸡腿 (zha ji tui)
→ fried chicken thighs

Korea
튀기다 (twigida)
Example: 닭 튀김 (dak twigim)
→ fried chicken

Pickle

Vietnam
Muối
Example: dưa muối
→ pickles

Thailand
ดอง (dong)
Example: ผักกาดดอง
(pak kad dong) → pickled
mustard greens

China
腌 (yan)
Example: 腌芥菜 (yan jiecai)
→ pickled mustard greens

Korea
담그다 (damgeuda)
Example: 매실 장아찌 (maesil
jang-ajji) → pickled plums
(umeboshi in Japanese)

Stir-fry

Vietnam
Xào
Example: gà xào sả ớt
→ chicken with lemongrass
and chili peppers

Thailand
ผัด (pad)
Example: ผัดซีอิ๊ว (pad
see ew) → stir-fried noodles

China
炒 (chao)
Example: 炒青菜 (chao qing
cai) → stir-fried greens

Korea
볶다 (bokkda)
Example: 떡볶이 (tteok-bokki)
→ stir-fried mochi rice cakes

Other terms to remember:

Vietnam quấn (to wrap), nấu (to cook, simmer), hấp (to steam), ngon (delicious)

Thailand ต้ม tom (to boil), เผ็ด phet (spicy), เปรี้ยว priao (sour), อร่อย aroi (delicious)

China 甜 tian (sweet), 辣 la (spicy), 咸 xian (salty), 好吃 hao chi (delicious)

Korea 굽다 gubda (to bake, cook), 졸이다 jol-ida (to cook, simmer), 찌다 jjida (to steam)
맛있다 masidda (delicious)

Asian Herb Heaven

From fresh coriander to basil, mint and lemongrass, herbs are essential to many Asian cuisines. Serve a heap of them to eat with meat or fish, and fill your senses with their fresh flavor. "Herb power" will make your body feel as if it's being renewed from the inside-out!

Fresh Asian herbs are widely available now but you can use dried herbs if you can't find fresh ones.

It's a seasoning and not an herb, but chili peppers are used often in these recipes.

Fresh coriander leaves (cilantro) is an indispensable herb in Asian cuisine. The plant with white roots shown on the facing page is coriander. I love this herb, and buy it cheaply in bulk at a local Asian grocery store. Coriander, referred to as *pak chi* in Thai and *yán sui* in Chinese, is popular not only in Southeast Asia, but also in China, India and many other countries around the region. Although some people dislike its distinctive fragrance, coriander is becoming increasingly popular around the world, too. If you visit Vietnam you will see this herb served in huge heaps, but you may find that difficult to do at home. You can still always enjoy this herb in small amounts by cutting it up finely to release the aroma.

Mint (pictured in the center of the facing page) and Thai basil, also called holy basil, aniseed basil or licorice basil (pictured in the bottom center) are commonly used in Thai and Vietnamese cuisines. When paired with deep-fried foods or stir-fried dishes with lots of flavor, they add a clean, refreshing finish. Lemongrass (pictured at left on the facing page), which is used in the popular Thai dish *Tom yum Goong*, has a distinct, crisply refreshing lemon-like aroma as you can tell from its name. The green leaves are often added to soups or stir-fries to add fragrance, but the roots actually have a stronger fragrance and can be eaten raw when chopped finely. I show you how to use lemongrass in this book.

If your herbs start to wilt, just wrap the roots in a paper towel and soak them in water, which will bring them back to vitality. Similarly, soaking greens such as Chinese spinach in water before stir-frying them will make them crisper after they're cooked.

If you don't have fresh herbs, you can still enjoy these Asian herbs through the judicious use of dried or powdered versions.

Chopping herbs makes them more fragrant.

Freshen up these leaves by letting them sit in a bowl of water for a while!

Drinks To Enjoy with Asian Salads

I really start craving beers from around Asia in the summer—they pair perfectly with flavor-packed Asian salads. I also recommend *makgeolli* (a milky, sparkling rice wine) from Korea and Shaoxing rice wine from China as alcoholic beverages that are great with these salads. What will you have to drink with your salad today?

Look for Asian cups and dishes in Asian markets to add a touch of authenticity to your presentation!

Packed with hot chili peppers, spices and fragrant herbs, many Asian salads pair perfectly with Asian beers. Each country has a variety of brands, but the most famous beers are 333 (pronounced *ba ba ba*), Saigon from Vietnam, Chang and Singha from Thailand and Tsingtao from China; they are all sold internationally. While each beer has a unique flavor of course, I think that Asian beers in general are refreshing and easy to drink, making them suitable to serve with almost any type of food. I also love the cool, refreshing sensation of swigging them down during hot weather and when eating spicy food. Salads that are flavored with spices, such as Vietnamese-style Fried Fish Cake and Herb Salad (see page 68), Fried Spring Rolls with Fresh Herbs (page 72), and Oven-baked Tandoori Chicken Salad (page 58) go particularly well with Asian beers.

Alcoholic beverages from around Asia such as *makgeolli* from Korea and Shaoxing wine from China are also sold worldwide. Makgeolli, with its gentle sweetness, subtle acidity and light carbonation, goes well with Korean salads such as Korean Perilla and Zha Cai Salad (page 29) and Spicy Marinated Tomatoes (page 18). Shaoxing wine has a complex aroma and rich flavor, making it a perfect drink to serve with simple salads such as Shredded Potato and Red Bell Pepper with Black Vinegar (page 34) and Stir-fried Green Asparagus and Lily Bulbs (page 86). I also introduce a variety of salads that go well with wine, sake, *shochu* (a Japanese alcoholic beverage of moderate strength, distilled from a variety of ingredients) and other alcoholic beverages, so I hope you'll use the recipes in this book to find the perfect salads to pair with your favorite drinks.

Asian beers and wines go really well with the recipes in this book!

For some reason, pouring beer into a small glass reminds me of Asia!

Hearty Salads with Rice or Noodles

Richly flavored, filling salads are perfect for serving over warm rice to make a delicious rice bowl. There are also many salads that compliment the Asian noodles that we have come to know and love, such as glass or cellophane noodles (rice vermicelli) or pho noodles. Can you guess what my favorite single-dish meal is?

Asian salads go really well with rice and noodles.

These convenient plastic rice-serving bowls were a souvenir from my trip to China.

Ceramic bowls with lids are also quite handy.

This book includes a variety of salads, from simple vegetable salads to make-in-advance pickled and marinated salads that are so handy to have on hand. All work well as side dishes, but I especially recommend putting hearty main dish salads that contain meat or seafood on top of rice to make a rice bowl. Richly flavored salads such as Pork, Kimchi and Leek Salad (see page 83), Chicken & Green Onion with Spicy Sesame Dressing (page 57), Fried Fish Nuggets with Carrots and Onion Chili Sauce (page 73), Sweet & Salty Pork and Water Spinach Stir-fry (page 84) and Stir-fried Chicken with Bamboo Shoots and Ginger (page 91) work really well as rice bowl toppings.

In addition, as I mention on the following page, putting the rice into tableware that I have bought on my trips, such as a bowl with a lid or the cheap but cute plastic bowls, really gives the meal an Asian vibe. There are a variety of rices too: glutinous rice, used commonly for red bean and rice dishes in China, Thai or Indica rice, which go well with Southeast Asian and Indian cuisines, and mixed grain rice, used commonly in Korea. You may enjoy exploring the variety of rices to find your favorites and discover which rice pairs with which cuisines.

Along with rice, noodles are also an essential part of Asian cuisine. While there is a variety of noodles, Chinese or Korean glass noodles (vermicelli) and Vietnamese pho are popular and can be bought worldwide. There are so many salads that pair superbly with noodles. For example, you can try stir-frying glass noodles with Fried Tofu and Bean Sprout Stir-fry (page 94), add pho to Thai Crispy Pork Salad (page 60) or serve Jellyfish and Cucumber Salad (page 50) over somen noodles, thin wheat noodles from Japan. I encourage you to try all kinds of combinations!

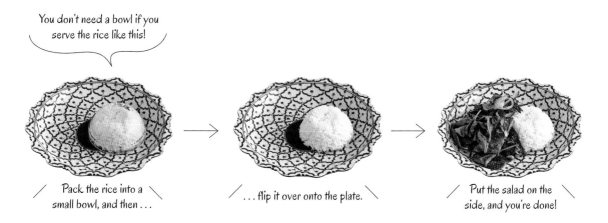

You don't need a bowl if you serve the rice like this!

Pack the rice into a small bowl, and then . . .

. . . flip it over onto the plate.

Put the salad on the side, and you're done!

Kitchen and Tableware From Around Asia

From the common and simple containers and cutlery to steamers and baskets, each country in Asia has its own set of unique kitchen utensils. I love looking around for wonderful items like these during my trips. I also use the kitchen utensils I have accumulated throughout my trips to make the Asian dishes that I cook look even more appetizing.

Striking colors! Chinese spoons and chopsticks are often red.

Southeast Asian utensils are often pink or blue.

Indian ones are often brass.

Wicker goods are found all over Asia.

I love traveling, and I often go to various countries around Asia. In addition to searching out ingredients, I also enjoy looking for kitchen utensils and tableware that typify the atmosphere of each country I'm visiting. Whenever I visit a country, I usually visit the markets, stores that sell items for the home, antique shops and so on. I have been visiting Taiwan every year for the past few years. I like to browse for Taiwanese-style tableware and tea sets in the Yingge district, a part of Taipei famous for its pottery. I also go looking for bargains at hardware stores in the more rural towns, and I've found cute plastic Chinese soup spoons and the like at the equivalent of dollar stores. I never get tired of looking for household items in Taiwan.

Vietnam, which I also visit frequently, is not to be outdone in the beauty of their tableware and household items. Bat Trang and Song Be pottery tableware is famous for being simple and convenient for everyday use. The Ben Thanh market in Ho Chi Minh City sells ingredients, kitchen utensils, clothes and more. It's so fun to look for souvenirs there.

The items that I have slowly accumulated are so useful when I set my table to serve dishes from around Asia. I like to serve deep-fried Thai or Vietnamese food in wicker baskets, and set out the simple Taiwanese or Vietnamese tableware that goes so well with them. Putting the bamboo steamer that I use all the time on the table instantly brings a Chinese flair. A Korean traditional *bojagi* cloth is a great accent for a dining table, and using the colorful utensils from the different countries creates the feeling that you are visiting that country. I think that contemplating what tableware to use and how to arrange food on it is just another way to enjoy Asian cuisine.

Using plates with matching designs creates that traveling vibe.

You can use a banana leaf as a serving plate too!

Lay a *bojagi* cloth on the table to transform your dining room into a little Korean eatery.

Versatile Asian Dressings

I have used these versatile dressings in several recipes in this book. Each recipe uses seasonings and ingredients commonly used in the respective country's cuisine. With these dressings on hand, you can easily bring the flavors of each country to your dinner table.

Vietnamese Nuoc Mam Dressing

MAKES ⅔ CUP

Finely mince 5 coriander stalks and 1 peeled garlic clove and put in a bowl. Add 1 tablespoon lemon juice, 4 tablespoons *nuoc mam*, and 2 tablespoons rice vinegar to the bowl. Mix well. Add 4 lemon slices.

*Keeps in the refrigerator for about 4 days.

Thai Nam Pla Dressing

MAKES ½ CUP

Peel and finely mince 1 garlic clove and one 1-inch (2.5-cm) piece of fresh ginger and put them in a bowl. Add 4 tablespoons *nam pla* and 2 tablespoons rice vinegar to the bowl. Mix well.

*Keeps in the refrigerator for about 5 days.

Indian Yogurt Dressing

MAKES 1 CUP

Put 1 scant cup (200 ml) plain unsweetened yogurt, 1 peeled and grated garlic clove, 1 teaspoon cumin powder, ⅓ teaspoon salt, a pinch of coarsely ground black pepper and 2 teaspoons olive oil in a bowl. Mix well.

*Keeps in the refrigerator for about 4 days.

Chinese Szechuan Pepper Dressing

MAKES ⅓ CUP

Put 2 teaspoons each Szechuan or Sichuan peppercorns and white sugar, ⅓ teaspoon salt, 2 tablespoons each of Shaoxing wine (or sake) and rice vinegar and 1 tablespoon sesame oil into a saucepan over medium heat. Take the pan off the heat when it comes to a boil and leave to cool.

*Keeps in the refrigerator for about 1 week.

Chinese Five Spice Dressing

MAKES ⅓ CUP

Peel and finely mince 1 garlic clove and one 1-inch (2.5-cm) piece of fresh ginger and put in a saucepan. Add 1 star anise, ½ teaspoon five spice powder, 3 tablespoons each black vinegar and soy sauce, and 2 tablespoons each Shaoxing wine (or sake) and mirin in a saucepan. Bring to a boil over medium heat, take off the heat and leave to cool.

*Keeps in the refrigerator for about 1 week.

Korean Gochujang Dressing

MAKES ¾ CUP

Put 2 teaspoons each *gochujang* and coarsely ground red pepper, 1 peeled and grated garlic clove, one 1-inch (2.5-cm) piece of peeled and grated fresh ginger, 2 tablespoons each of roasted white sesame seeds and sesame oil and 4 tablespoons each of black vinegar and soy sauce into a bowl and mix well.

*Keeps in the refrigerator for about 1 week.

Chapter 1
Marinated and Pickled Salads

Gochujang, spices, *nam pla*, and *nuoc mam* and more—these flavoring ingredients represent the allure of each Asian country's cuisine. In this chapter you'll find make-ahead marinated or pickled salads that highlight the unique characteristics of these flavors. If you have some of these in stock, you can easily add a flavor of Asia to your dinner table whenever you want.

Marinated Turnip and Tomato Salad (photo on facing page)

This marinated salad has very aromatic dressing with Szechuan pepper, sesame oil and Shaoxing wine.

SERVES 2
PREP TIME: 15 MINUTES
MARINATING TIME: 30 MINUTES

2 small Asian turnips (available at Asian grocery stores)
⅓ teaspoon salt
1 large tomato

A
- 2 tablespoons Chinese Szechuan Pepper Dressing (see page 15)
- One 1-inch (2.5-cm) piece fresh ginger, peeled and thinly sliced

DIRECTIONS

1 Cut off all but ¾ inch (2 cm) of the stems from the turnips and cut them into 10 wedges each. Sprinkle with salt and leave for 10 minutes. Pat dry with a paper towel.
2 Cut the tomato into 8 wedges.
3 Combine the ingredients in **A** in a bowl. Add the ingredients from Steps **1** and **2** and mix.
   *This dish tastes best after marinating for around 30 minutes. It keeps in the refrigerator for about 2 days.

Marinated Bean Sprouts with Black Vinegar Dressing

This is a simple salad made with just bean sprouts and dressing. Black vinegar, with its full-bodied fragrance and mellow sourness, is the key to this dish.

SERVES 2
PREP TIME: 15 MINUTES
MARINATING TIME: 30 MINUTES

8 oz (250 g) bean sprouts

A
- ½ fresh red chili pepper (seeds removed and chopped)
- 1 tablespoon white sugar
- 3 tablespoons black vinegar
- 1½ tablespoons soy sauce
- ½ cup (120 ml) water

DIRECTIONS

1 Remove the thin roots from the bean sprouts. Rinse the sprouts and drain them thoroughly. Put them in a tightly sealing heatproof storage container.
2 Put the ingredients in **A** in a saucepan and heat over medium heat. When it comes a boil, pour over the bean sprouts while still hot.
   *Best after being marinating for about 30 minutes. It keeps in the refrigerator for about 2 days.

Spicy Marinated Tomatoes

This spicy and complex marinade contains *gochujang* (Korean fermented chili paste), black vinegar and aromatic vegetables. It really brings out the sweetness of the tomatoes. Hot sesame oil also elevates the flavor and aroma of the dish.

SERVES 2 TO 3
PREP TIME: 10 MINUTES
MARINATING TIME: 30 MINUTES

10 large cherry tomatoes (tomatoes on the vine are perfect for this dish)

A
- **¼ green onion (scallion), finely chopped**
- **One ½-inch (1.25-cm) piece fresh ginger, peeled and finely chopped**
- **1 teaspoon *gochujang***
- **1 tablespoon black vinegar**
- **2 teaspoons soy sauce**

2 tablespoons sesame oil

DIRECTIONS

1 Make crisscross incisions with a knife in the bottom end of each tomato, but don't cut all the way through.

2 Dunk the tomatoes in boiling water for about 20 seconds (see photo a). Take them out and plunge them immediately into cold water. Peel off the skin and remove the calyxes. Pat dry with a paper towel, and then cut each tomato in half lengthwise.

3 Combine the ingredients in **A** in a bowl and mix well (see photo b). Put the peeled tomatoes from Step **2** into the bowl and mix.

4 Heat the sesame oil in a saucepan over medium-low heat. When it's hot, add it to the bowl from Step **3**, mixing to evenly coat the tomatoes with the oil and marinade (see photo c).

*Marinate for around 30 minutes for the best results. This will keep in the refrigerator for about 4 days.

These *gochujang* marinated tomatoes complement the slight acidity of *makgeolli* (a milky, sparkling rice wine) well. The combination is perfect for sipping and nibbling.

a

b

c

TIP I marinated some large, fruity cherry tomatoes in a mixture that includes *gochujang*, an essential ingredient in Korean cooking, and aromatic vegetables. The marinade is also wonderful when used with other vegetables, such as cucumbers and red bell peppers, as well as with seafood such as boiled octopus or raw tuna. The key to maximizing the flavor is to heat up the sesame oil before adding it to the marinade.

Spicy Pickled Napa Cabbage and Baby Carrots

A few days after this dish is made, the cabbage's sweetness grows more noticeable as the sourness mellows out. You can enjoy this dish as its flavors change over time.

SERVES 2 TO 3
PREP TIME: 10 MINUTES
MARINATING TIME: 12–24 HOURS

¼ head napa cabbage
4 baby carrots (or 1 large carrot)

A
- ½ fresh red chili pepper (seeds removed and chopped)
- 2 tablespoons white sugar
- ⅔ teaspoon salt
- ¼ cup (65 ml) Shaoxing wine (or sake)
- 2 tablespoons black vinegar
- ⅔ cup (160 ml) water

DIRECTIONS

1 Slice the napa cabbage in half lengthwise and then into 4 equal-size pieces. Cut the carrots in half lengthwise (see photo a). (If you're using a large carrot, cut it into 2 x ⅓-inch / 5-cm x 5-mm sticks.) Put the cabbage and carrots in a tightly sealing heatproof storage container.

2 Put the ingredients in **A** in a saucepan and heat over medium heat (see photo b). When it comes to a boil, simmer for about 1 minute. Pour the liquid over the ingredients in Step **1** while still hot (see photo c). Cool to room temperature, then marinate in the refrigerator.
*This tastes best after half a day to a full day. It will keep in the refrigerator for about 2 weeks.

A non-reactive glass container works well for this recipe. If you're using a deeper container, put the thicker parts of the napa cabbage close to the bottom to pickle them more effectively.

a

b

c

TIP Called "辣白菜" (la bai cai), this typical Chinese side dish is made by pickling napa cabbage in vinegar seasoned with red chili peppers. Here I've added some cute baby carrots. This dish tastes best when the napa cabbage is cut into larger pieces and left to marinate for about half a day to a whole day. Because it keeps for some time, it's really handy to have on hand.

Pickled Daikon Radish and Carrot Salad

This is so simple to make yet has complex flavors, with the sweetness of the daikon radish and carrots, the umami of *nuoc mam*, and the spiciness of green chili peppers.

SERVES 2
PREP TIME: 15 MINUTES
MARINATING TIME: 30 MINUTES

1 fresh green chili pepper

A ⌈ 1 teaspoon white sugar
  │ 1 ½ tablespoons *nuoc mam*
  └ 1 tablespoon rice vinegar

10½ oz (300 g) daikon radish

1 medium carrot

⅔ teaspoon salt

DIRECTIONS

1 Cut the green chili pepper in half lengthwise. Combine with the ingredients in **A** in a bowl. Mix thoroughly and leave to rest for 10 minutes.

2 Finely shred the daikon radish and carrot. Mix them together and sprinkle with salt. Rub the salt in until the daikon radish and carrots become wilted. Leave for 5 minutes and then firmly squeeze out the moisture. Add to the bowl in Step **1** and mix to combine.

*This dish tastes best after marinating for about 30 minutes. It keeps in the refrigerator for about 1 week.

....

TIP This Vietnamese vegetable dish features daikon radish and carrots marinated in a sweet and sour *nuoc mam* sauce. It is an essential side dish in Vietnamese cuisine, and is often used in banh mi sandwiches or as a garnish for other dishes. You can also add texture and flavor by scattering on some peanuts. Make sure you squeeze the moisture out of the daikon radish and carrots thoroughly after you rub in the salt.

Marinated Cucumber with Garlic and Nuoc Mam

The clean spiciness of the fresh chili pepper and the flavor of the garlic really work well in this simple marinated salad. You'll want to have this stocked in your refrigerator often.

SERVES 2
PREP TIME: 10 MINUTES
MARINATING TIME: 12 HOURS

A
- ½ **fresh red chili pepper, de-seeded and thinly sliced**
- 1 **clove garlic, peeled and crushed**
- 1 **teaspoon white sugar**
- 2 **tablespoons *nuoc mam***
- 2 **tablespoons rice vinegar**

2 **small or 1 large cucumber**
½ **teaspoon salt**

DIRECTIONS

1 Mix the ingredients in **A** together in a tightly sealing storage container.
2 Sprinkle the cucumber with salt, then roll it around several times on a cutting board to really rub the salt in well. Wipe the excess salt off the cucumber with a paper towel. Cut into 1 inch (3 cm) long pieces.
Marinate the cucumber in the mixture made in Step **1**.
*This tastes best after being left to rest for about half a day. It keeps in the refrigerator for about 1 week.

....

TIP *Nuoc mam is an essential seasoning ingredient in Vietnamese cuisine. Its strong aroma and saltiness make it very distinctive. This simple marinade is inspired by other nuoc-mam-based marinated vegetable dishes. You can use this for other vegetables such as daikon radishes, carrots or celery. Try it with whatever vegetables you have left over in your refrigerator.*

Salted Napa Cabbage with Coriander and Chili Oil

This dish packs a punch from the spicy homemade chili oil. I highly recommend having a beer with this.

SERVES 2 TO 3
PREP TIME: 10 MINUTES
MARINATING TIME: 30 MINUTES

⅙ **head napa cabbage**

⅓ **teaspoon salt**

4 stalks fresh coriander

A
- **1 clove garlic, peeled and finely chopped**
- ⅓ **teaspoon chili pepper powder**
- **2 tablespoons Shaoxing wine (or sake)**
- **1 tablespoon black vinegar**
- **1 teaspoon soy sauce**
- **2 teaspoons sesame oil**

DIRECTIONS

1 Slice the napa cabbage into ⅓ inch (1 cm) wide pieces and sprinkle with salt. Rub the salt in well until the cabbage is wilted. Firmly squeeze out the excess moisture.

2 Roughly chop the coriander, and mix with the salted napa cabbage. Arrange on a serving plate.

3 Heat the ingredients in **A** in a saucepan over medium-low heat. When it comes to a boil, pour over the plate prepared in Step **2**.
   *This dish tastes best if left to marinate for about 30 minutes. It keeps in the refrigerator for about 1 week.

Dried Tofu and Seaweed Salad with Black Vinegar

The pickling juice seeps into the mild dried tofu, making it smooth like noodles. You won't be able to stop eating it.

SERVES 2
PREP TIME: 15 MINUTES
MARINATING TIME: 1 HOUR

3½ oz (90 g) dried tofu (see page 6)

¼ oz (10 g) *kombu* seaweed strips
(Available at Japanese grocery stores.
If you can't find strips, cut whole
leaves of *kombu* seaweed into thin
strips with kitchen scissors.)

A
┌ 1 tablespoon roasted white sesame
│   seeds
│ 1 tablespoon soy sauce
│ 1 pinch salt
└ 2 tablespoons black vinegar

2 teaspoons sesame oil

DIRECTIONS

1 Cook the dried tofu in boiling water for 2 minutes. Drain well and cut into easy-to-eat pieces.

2 Soak the *kombu* strips in water for 10 minutes or more until soft (you may need to soak cut-up whole *kombu* for an hour or more). Drain thoroughly and cut into easy-to-eat lengths if needed.

3 Combine the ingredients in **A** in a bowl. Add in the ingredients from Steps **1** and **2** and mix to evenly coat the ingredients. Swirl in the sesame oil and toss quickly to coat.

*This dish tastes best if marinated for about 1 hour. It keeps in the refrigerator for about 3 days.

Sweet Pickled Red Onions

These pickles have a beautiful color and a refreshing acidity. You can also taste the sweetness and spiciness of the onions.

MAKES 1 JAR, ENOUGH FOR
   SEVERAL SERVINGS
PREP TIME: 10 MINUTES
MARINATING TIME: 2 HOURS

1 red onion

A
- 1 clove garlic, peeled and crushed
- 2 teaspoons cumin seeds
- 1 teaspoon salt
- 1 tablespoon white sugar (or caster sugar)
- ¼ cup (65 ml) white wine
- 2 tablespoons fresh lemon juice
- ¾ cup (185 ml) water

DIRECTIONS

1 Cut the red onion into ¾-inch (2-cm) dice and put into a non-reactive, tightly sealing container.

2 Heat the ingredients in **A** in a saucepan over medium heat. Bring to a boil, and simmer for one minute. Pour the liquid into the container over the onions from Step 1 while it is still hot.

*This dish tastes best after marinating for about 2 hours. It keeps in the refrigerator for about 2 weeks.

TIP   This cumin-scented pickle is quite sour due to the strong acidity of lemon juice. It can be used in many ways; as a garnish for curry, as a salad topping and more.

Pickled Chickpeas and Kidney Beans

The spices and the acidity of the apple cider vinegar brings out the sweetness of the beans. So delicious!

MAKES ONE JAR, ENOUGH FOR SEVERAL SERVINGS
PREP TIME: 5 MINUTES
MARINATING TIME: 2 HOURS

3½ oz (90 g) cooked chickpeas

3½ oz (90 g) cooked kidney beans

A ⎰ 1 clove garlic, peeled and crushed
1 bay leaf
¼ teaspoon *garam masala*
1 teaspoon curry powder
1 teaspoon salt
Scant ¼ cup (50 ml) white wine
Scant ½ cup (100 ml) each apple cider vinegar and water

DIRECTIONS

1 Put the chickpeas and kidney beans in a non-reactive, tightly sealing container.

2 Heat the ingredients in **A** in a saucepan. Bring to a boil and simmer for 1 minute. Pour the liquid into the container over the beans from Step **1** while still hot. *This dish tastes best after it has marinated for about 2 hours. It keeps in the refrigerator for about 2 weeks.

TIP These flavorful pickled beans are infused with the sweet-sour flavors of apple cider vinegar and spicy *garam masala*. It's a great snack to nibble on when you're sipping a drink.

Chapter 2
Light and Refreshing Salads

From simple salads using familiar vegetables that are quickly tossed with a dressing to filling main dish salads, this chapter includes a variety of vegetable salads inspired by several Asian cuisines. Packed with fresh herbs, acidity and spice, these salads make frequent appearances on my dinner table when the weather is hot.

Korean Perilla and Zha Cai Salad (photo on facing page)

Perilla, a close relation to the Japanese green shiso, is a staple ingredient in Korean cuisine. I've added salty *zha cai* pickles to make it a salad that works well as a drinking appetizer.

SERVES 2
PREP TIME: 10 MINUTES

¼ cup (60 g) *zha cai* pickles (*Zha cai* is a salty pickle from Szechuan province in China made with mustard plant stems. It's available at Asian grocery stores.)
6 Korean perilla leaves
1 oz (30 g) radish sprouts
1 tablespoon Korean Gochujang Dressing (see page 15)

DIRECTIONS

1 Rinse the *zha cai* briefly and chop finely. Soak in water for 10 minutes to remove the brine. Pat dry with a paper towel and cut into thin matchsticks.
2 Tear the Korean perilla leaves into easy-to-eat pieces. Remove the thin roots from the radish sprouts.
3 Put the Steps **1** and **2** ingredients in a bowl. Add the dressing and toss to combine.

Lettuce and Korean Nori Seaweed Salad

This recipe is based on *sangchu-geotjeori*, a salad popular at Korean barbecue restaurants. In South Korea the grilled meat is often wrapped in *sangchu* or loose leaf lettuce, the star of this dish.

SERVES 2
PREP TIME: 10 MINUTES

6 red or green loose leaf lettuce leaves
6 green onions (scallions)
A ⌈ 1 tablespoon black vinegar
  ⌊ 2 teaspoons soy sauce
6 sheets Korean nori seaweed (available at Korean grocery stores)
2 teaspoons sesame oil

DIRECTIONS

1 Tear the lettuce into easy-to-eat sizes. Cut the green onion into 2 inch (5 cm) long pieces.
2 Combine the ingredients in **A** in a bowl. Add the lettuce and green onions and toss. Tear the nori seaweed into easy-to-eat pieces and add it to the bowl. Drizzle in the sesame oil and toss quickly to combine.

Tomato and Bean Sprouts with Vietnamese Dressing

Just toss everyday vegetables with a flavorful dressing. This salad is so simple, and makes a great side dish.

SERVES 2
PREP TIME: 10 MINUTES

10 cherry tomatoes

8 oz (250 g) soy bean sprouts

3 tablespoons Vietnamese Nuoc Mam
    Dressing (see page 15)

DIRECTIONS

1 Cut the cherry tomatoes in half lengthwise.
2 Remove the thin roots from the bean sprouts. Put the sprouts in a colander and pour boiling water over them. Drain well.
3 Put the tomatoes and bean sprouts in a bowl. Add the dressing and toss quickly.

TIP Bean sprouts are a staple ingredient in Vietnamese cuisine, used in dishes such as pho and *banh xeo*. Bean sprouts are typically just used raw in Vietnam, but I prefer to pour boiling water over them to remove the grassy smell.

Coriander and Water Spinach with Lime and Nuoc Mam Dressing

This salad uses aromatic vegetables and Thai flavors. This easy dish has a simple appearance, but a captivating taste.

SERVES 2
PREP TIME: 10 MINUTES

1 bunch (about 3½ oz / 90 g) fresh coriander
1 bunch (about 3½ oz / 90 g) water spinach
   (Water spinach, also called water dropwort, *kangkong*
   or *seri*, is available at Asian grocery stores. See Tip
   for substitution suggestions.)

A
- ½ fresh red chili pepper, de-seeded and chopped
- 8 half-moon-shaped lime slices (4 slices cut in half)
- 1 tablespoon fresh lime juice
- 2 tablespoons *nuoc mam*

DIRECTIONS

1 Cut the roots off the coriander and water spinach, and chop into 1½-inch (4-cm) pieces.
2 Mix the ingredients in **A** in a bowl. Add the ingredients from Step **1** toss quickly.

TIP Fresh coriander, an indispensable ingredient in so many Asian cuisines, is the star of this salad that's flavored with lime and the distinctive flavor of *nuoc mam*. If you can't find water spinach, you can substitute edible chrysanthemum leaves, *mizuna* greens or spinach leaves.

Cucumber Salad with Yogurt & Garlic Dressing Raita

Combining the acidity of yogurt with the flavor of grated garlic, this dressing is simple yet so addictive. It goes so well with the cucumber.

SERVES 2
PREP TIME: 10 MINUTES

1 small cucumber

A
- Scant ½ cup (100 ml) plain unsweetened yogurt
- 1 clove garlic, peeled and grated
- ¼ teaspoon salt

1 tablespoon olive oil
Red chili pepper powder, to taste (optional)

DIRECTIONS

1 Cut the cucumber in half lengthwise and remove the seeds. Roughly chop up.
2 Combine the ingredients in **A** in a bowl, and add the cucumber. Add the olive oil and mix. Transfer to serving bowls, and optionally sprinkle with some red chili powder.

TIP   Raita is a standard salad in Indian cuisine. It's basically a salad made with vegetables or fruit, with a yogurt-based dressing. When eaten as a side dish, it makes spicy dishes such as curries milder. I have used cucumber here, but you can also use onions, tomatoes, beans, or even fruits such as apples or bananas. You can also combine multiple vegetables or fruit for delicious results.

Tomato, Cucumber and Onion Salad Kachumber

Scented with lemon and cumin, this is a very refreshing, crunchy salad. This is an excellent side dish for curries, and also works well as a cold pasta topping.

SERVES 2
PREP TIME: 15 MINUTES

1 small cucumber
½ red onion
½ teaspoon salt
1 medium tomato
4 stalks fresh coriander, finely chopped
A ⌈ ⅓ teaspoon cumin powder
  ⌊ 1 tablespoon fresh lemon juice
1 tablespoon olive oil
Ground cumin, to taste (optional)

DIRECTIONS

1 Slice the cucumber in half lengthwise, and remove the seeds. Cut it in half lengthwise again, and then chop it into ⅓-inch (1-cm) pieces. Cut the red onion into ⅓-inch (1-cm) dice.

2 Mix the ingredients from Step **1** with the salt in a bowl. Leave for 10 minutes, then drain thoroughly.

3 Cut the tomato into ⅓-inch (1-cm) dice. Put the tomato and the ingredients from **A** into the bowl from Step **2**, and mix thoroughly. Drizzle in the olive oil and toss quickly. Transfer to serving bowls, and optionally sprinkle with ground cumin.

TIP Like raita, *kachumber* is a standard salad in India. Packed with spices, it exemplifies Indian cuisine. Cucumber and tomatoes are usually used, but there are also recipes that add celery or beans, so you can vary the ingredients to your taste. Chili powder would be a great addition to make this spicy-hot. *Kachumber* is often served as a side dish as part of the multi-dish meal set that's become so popular at South Indian restaurants in Japan recently.

Shredded Potato and Red Bell Pepper with Black Vinegar

This simple tossed salad highlights the complex flavor of black vinegar. The sprinkle of five spice powder added at the end makes it taste very Chinese. The potato is cooked very briefly to retain its crunchy texture.

SERVES 2

PREP TIME: 10 MINUTES

3 medium potatoes

1 tablespoon Shaoxing wine (or sake)

2 small red bell peppers

A ⌈ 1 tablespoon black vinegar
  ⌊ 2 teaspoons *nam pla*

2 teaspoons sesame oil

1 pinch five spice powder

DIRECTIONS

1 Peel and finely shred the potatoes, and soak in a bowl of cold water for a minute. Drain. Bring a pan of water to a boil with the Shaoxing wine and add the shredded potatoes. Boil for 45 seconds, then drain well.

2 De-seed and thinly slice the bell peppers lengthwise, and soak in a bowl of cold water for about 3 minutes. Drain well.

3 Mix the ingredients in **A** in a bowl, add the potato and bell pepper, and toss well to coat. Drizzle in the sesame oil and mix. Transfer to serving plates, and sprinkle with a little five spice powder.

Steamed Eggplant with Szechuan Pepper Dressing

The unique tongue-numbing spiciness of the Szechuan pepper perfectly complements the soft steamed eggplant. Chopped fresh coriander adds a nice accent.

SERVES 2 TO 3
PREP TIME: 15 MINUTES
COOKING TIME: 10 MINUTES

5 small Japanese eggplants or 3 thin Chinese eggplants

A
- **1 teaspoon ground Szechuan pepper**
- **1 tablespoon roasted white sesame seeds**
- **1 tablespoon Shaoxing wine (or sake)**
- **1 tablespoon sesame oil**
- **2 tablespoons black vinegar**
- **2 tablespoons soy sauce**

4 stalks fresh coriander
One 1-inch (2.5-cm) piece fresh ginger, peeled and finely chopped

DIRECTIONS

1 Peel the eggplants, soak them in cold water for 3 minutes, and then drain well. Place in a steamer and steam over high heat for about 10 minutes.

2 Heat the ingredients in **A** in a saucepan over medium heat until it comes to a boil.

3 Cut the steamed eggplant into 1-inch (2.5-cm) pieces. Arrange on a plate and garnish with roughly chopped coriander and the ginger. Pour on the dressing from Step **2**.

Century Egg Salad with Tomato and Celery

The rich, complex flavor of the century egg, acidity of the tomato, and the full-bodied aroma of the black vinegar complement each other perfectly in this striking salad.

SERVES 2
PREP TIME: 10 MINUTES
EGG REST TIME: 12 HOURS

1 century egg or *pidan* (see page 6)
1 large tomato
½ celery stalk
4 fresh coriander stalks

A
┌ 1 clove garlic, peeled and thinly
│   sliced
│ 1 tablespoon black vinegar
└ 1 teaspoon soy sauce

1 tablespoon sesame oil

DIRECTIONS

1 Shell the century egg and place it in a bowl. Cover the bowl loosely with plastic wrap, and refrigerate it overnight to eliminate the odor.

2 Cut the tomato and the egg into 1-inch (3-cm) dice. Remove the tough strings from the celery and slice thinly.

3 Roughly chop the coriander.

4 Mix the ingredients together in **A** in a bowl. Add the ingredients from Step **2** and toss quickly to coat them with the dressing. Add the coriander, swirl in the sesame oil and mix briefly.

··

TIP   Century egg is often put into rice porridge in Taiwan. Because dishes that include fresh coriander are also very common there, I thought up this dish that uses both ingredients together with tomato and celery.

Cloud Ear Mushroom and Cucumber Salad

This light and refreshing dish is made with a ginger-accented, oil-free vinegar sauce. The crunchy texture of the cloud ear mushrooms is irresistible!

SERVES 2
PREP TIME: 25 MINUTES

1 oz (30 g) dried white cloud ear mushrooms (also called white fungus or snow fungus)

2 small or 1 large cucumber

⅓ teaspoon salt

A {
- One 1-inch (2.5-cm) piece fresh ginger, peeled and shredded
- 2 teaspoons roasted white sesame seeds
- 2 tablespoons black vinegar
- 1 tablespoon soy sauce
}

2 teaspoons sesame oil

DIRECTIONS

1 Soak the cloud ear mushrooms in warm water for 20 minutes. Remove the tough stems and tear into easy- to-eat pieces. Cook the mushrooms in boiling water for 1 minute, and then drain well.

2 Make several cuts about two thirds of the way through the cucumber $1/16$ inch (2 mm) apart. Be careful not to cut all the way through the cucumber. Flip the cucumber over and repeat on the other side. (This cutting method is called the "bellows cut.") Sprinkle the cucumber with salt and rub it in. Leave until wilted, then cut up the cucumber into 1 inch (2.5 cm) long pieces.

3 Combine the ingredients in **A** into a bowl. Add the mushrooms and cucumber and toss together quickly. Add the sesame oil and mix briefly.

....

TIP I love a Taiwanese dessert made by simmering white cloud ear mushrooms in syrup, so I buy dried white cloud ear mushrooms every time I visit Taiwan. Here I've combined them with cucumber and flavored them with a light vinegar sauce.

Yam and Lotus Root Salad Namul

Namul is a standard Korean side dish consisting of various vegetables dressed with salt and sesame oil. Use whatever vegetables you have on hand, such as bean sprouts or various blanched greens.

SERVES 2
PREP TIME: 15 MINUTES
COOKING TIME: 1 MINUTE

5 oz (150 g) Chinese yam (also called
   ***nagaimo* or cinnamon root)**
1 teaspoon rice vinegar, divided
5 oz (150 g) lotus root
A ⌈ **⅓ teaspoon salt**
  ⌊ **2 teaspoons sesame oil**
Ground black sesame seeds, to taste

DIRECTIONS

1 Scrub the yam well using a stiff vegetable brush. Do not peel. Cut the yam into ⅛ inch (3 mm) thick rounds. Put the yam slices in a bowl and add enough water to cover plus ½ teaspoon of rice vinegar. Soak for 5minutes, and drain well.

2 Peel the lotus root, cut into ⅛ inch (3 mm) thick rounds, and soak in water briefly. Bring a pan of water to a boil and add the remaining ½ teaspoon of the vinegar. Put in the lotus root and boil for about 1 minute. Drain well.

3 Combine the ingredients in **A** in a bowl. Add the yam and lotus root, and toss to coat them in the sauce. Transfer to serving plates, and sprinkle with ground black sesame seeds.

TIP Some people have a mild allergic reaction to raw Chinese yam when they are handling it. If your hands feel itchy, use kitchen gloves or hold the yam with a plastic bag.

Green Papaya Salad Som Tam

Variations of this crunchy green papaya salad are eaten all over Southeast Asia. They're getting very popular around the world too. I like the fact that it's so easy to make if I have the dressing on hand.

SERVES 2
PREP TIME: 15 MINUTES
COOKING TIME: 5 MINUTES

1 green (unripe) papaya
4 green beans
½ medium carrot
6 yellow cherry tomatoes
½ fresh red chili pepper (de-seeded and chopped)
3 tablespoons Thai Nam Pla Dressing (see page 15)
1 tablespoon sesame oil

DIRECTIONS

1 Peel the green papaya and shred finely. Soak briefly in a bowl of cold water, and drain well.

2 Cut the ends off the green beans. Cook in boiling water for about 2 minutes, and drain well (keep the boiling water for the next step). Cut into thin diagonal slices.

3 Finely shred the carrot and put into the boiling water after removing the green beans in Step 2. Cook for 30 seconds, then drain well. Cut the cherry tomatoes in half lengthwise.

4 Combine all the vegetables from Steps 1–3 in a bowl with the red chili pepper. Add the dressing and toss well. Drizzle in the sesame oil and mix quickly.

Chapter 3
Seafood Salads

Seafood is popular throughout Asia. This section includes salads that work as side salads, as part of a multi-course meal, or on their own as main dish salads. I have used familiar seafood like shrimp, as well as items that may be less familiar to you as salad ingredients such as salted jellyfish and steamed clams.

Shrimp and Chicken Spring Rolls

These fresh-tasting spring rolls from Vietnam, made with rice paper and filled with vegetables and herbs, are like individual small salads.

MAKES 6 ROLLS
PREP TIME: 30 MINUTES
COOKING TIME: 5 MINUTES

2 tablespoons sake, divided
6 large shrimp, peeled, de-veined and heads removed
2 chicken tenderloins, about 4 oz (100 g)
⅔ oz (20 g) glass or cellophane noodles
4 leaves lettuce
3 thin green onions (scallions)
6 rice paper wrappers for spring rolls
6 fresh coriander stalks
Loose leaf lettuce and carrot sticks, for garnish
2 tablespoons sweet chili sauce

DIRECTIONS

1   Bring two pans of water to a boil, and add 1 tablespoon of sake to each pan. Boil the shrimp in one pan and the chicken in the other for about 2 minutes. Turn off the heat and leave the shrimp and chicken to cool. Drain and pat dry with paper towels. Slice the shrimp in half lengthwise, and shred the chicken into fairly large pieces.

2   Put the glass noodles into a bowl and pour just enough boiling water over them to submerge them. Leave them to soak for 10 minutes until the noodles are tender, and then drain well. Shred the lettuce, and cut the green onions into 2 inch (5 cm) long pieces.

3   Place the rice paper wrappers on sheets of waxed paper, and spray the wrappers with water until they are softened. Place the shrimp along the middle of three of the rice paper wrappers and the chicken in the middle of the three other wrappers. Put coriander on all the wrappers.

4   Place some glass noodles and green onions on the edge closest to you on each wrapper. Roll up the wrappers once, fold in the sides and then finish rolling them up. Cut into halves and arrange on serving plates, with the loose leaf lettuce, carrot sticks and chili sauce on the side.

Squid and Celery Salad with Spicy Thai Dressing

When you finish cooking squid in residual heat, it turns out to be very tender and moist. The soft squid contrasts well with the crunchiness of the celery. I never get tired of this salad.

SERVES 2
PREP TIME: 20 MINUTES
COOKING TIME: 20 MINUTES
MARINATING TIME: 30 MINUTES

2 raw squid

2 tablespoons sake

1 celery stalk

5 celery leaves

⅓ teaspoon salt

A
- **½ fresh green chili pepper, de-seeded and finely chopped**
- **2 tablespoons Thai Nam Pla Dressing (see page 15)**
- **2 tablespoons fresh lime juice**
- **1 tablespoon sesame oil**

DIRECTIONS

1 Remove the innards, ear flaps (the triangular bits on the side), legs, and quill from the squid, and peel off the skin. You should have about 7 ounces (200 g) of squid body. Slice the squid body into ¼ to ⅓ inch wide rings. Bring a pan of water to a boil, add the sake, and boil the squid for about 90 seconds. Turn off the heat, cover the pan with a lid, and leave the squid to cook in the residual heat. Take out the squid and drain well.

2 Remove the tough outer strings from the celery, and cut into ¼ inch (5 mm) wide pieces. Shred the leaves. Combine the celery stalk and leaves, and sprinkle with the salt. Rub it in until the celery is wilted, let rest for 5 minutes, and then squeeze out the excess moisture.

3 Combine the ingredients in **A** in a bowl. Add the ingredients from Steps **1** and **2**, and mix together.
*This dish is best when left to marinate for about 30 minutes. It will keep in the refrigerator for about 2 weeks.

....

TIP I love the combination of squid and celery, so they appear frequently on my dinner table, but it is also a common combination in Thai cuisine. This dish can be made quickly if you make the Thai Nam Pla Dressing (see page 15) in advance. The dressing can be used as-is, but you can also turn it into a marinade by adding ingredients such as sesame oil and lime juice, as I have done in this recipe.

Lemongrass and Seafood Salad

Lemongrass is called *takrai* in Thai. The key to this salad is to chop up and add the strongly fragrant base of the lemongreass.

SERVES 2
PREP TIME: 30 MINUTES
COOKING TIME: 20 MINUTES

- 2 small squid (spear squid, Pacific flying squid, etc.)
- 6 large shrimp (black tiger shrimp, whiteleg shrimp, etc.)
- 2 tablespoons potato starch or cornstarch
- 2 tablespoons sake
- Two 8-inch (20-cm) pieces lemongrass
- 2 tablespoons Thai Nam Pla Dressing (see page 15)
- ⅙ cabbage, shredded
- 4 fresh coriander stalks, roughly chopped
- 2 teaspoons sesame oil

DIRECTIONS

1. Remove the innards, ear flaps (the triangular bits on the side), legs, and quill from the squid, and peel off the skin. Reserve the legs. You should have about 6 to 7 ounces (180 to 200 g) of squid body and legs. Cut the squid bodies open so they lie flat, and slice into ⅓-inch (1-cm) strips. Chop up the legs into easy-to-eat pieces. De-vein the shrimp, sprinkle with potato starch or cornstarch, rub the starch into the shrimp and rinse off. (This cleans the shrimp.)
2. Bring a pan of water to a boil and add the sake. Put in the squid and shrimp and cook for 90 seconds. Turn off the heat, cover the pan with a lid, and continue to cook the squid and shrimp with residual heat. When they are cooked through, take out and drain well. Peel the shrimp.
3. Mince the lemongrass finely and soak in water for 3 minutes. Drain well.
4. Put the lemongrass and dressing in a bowl. Add the ingredients from Step **2** and mix well to coat with the dressing. Arrange on a serving plate with the cabbage on the side. Add the coriander and drizzle with the sesame oil.

Shrimp and Cucumber with Spicy Cashews

The nutty flavors of the deep-fried shrimp and cashews really make this dish. It's great snack to have with a drink.

SERVES 2
PREP TIME: 10 MINUTES
COOKING TIME: 5 MINUTES

10 to 12 medium shrimp (such as whiteleg shrimp) in their shells
3 fresh green chili peppers
1 small cucumber
Oil for deep frying
10 cashews
3 tablespoons Thai Nam Pla Dressing (see page 15)

DIRECTIONS

1 De-vein the shrimp and remove the whiskers. Make 2 to 3 lengthwise incisions in each green chili pepper with the tip of your knife.
2 Roughly cut up the cucumber.
3 Heat some oil in a pan to 340°F (170°C). Put in the cashews and fry until lightly browned. Remove the nuts and drain. Put the shrimp in the oil and fry until crispy, about 2 minutes.
4 Mix the ingredients from Steps **2** and **3** in a bowl. Add the dressing and toss well.

Mackerel Salad with Peanut Dressing

This is my version of a Thai salad called *Yum Pla Tu*. The salty mackerel and peanut sauce work surprisingly well together.

SERVES 2 TO 3
PREP TIME: 20 MINUTES
COOKING TIME: 5 TO 10 MINUTES

2 semi-dried horse mackerel, about 7 oz (200 g) (called *aji no himono*, available at Japanese grocery stores; or substitute smoked mackerel)
½ red onion
4 oz (100 g) bean sprouts
1 cup (20 g) mint leaves, loosely packed

A
- **3 tablespoons unsweetened peanut butter**
- **1 teaspoon dried red chili pepper flakes**
- **2 tablespoons fresh lemon juice**
- **1 tablespoon *nam pla***

Additional dried red chili pepper flakes, to taste

DIRECTIONS

1 Cook the mackerel on a grill for 8 to 10 minutes, or in a dry frying pan over medium heat for 5 to 6 minutes, turning once. Shred and remove any bones and skin while still warm. If using smoked mackerel, shred and remove any bones and skin.

2 Slice the red onion thinly lengthwise. Put the onions into a bowl of cold water for 3 minutes, then drain well. Remove the thin roots from the bean sprouts and put into a colander. Pour boiling water over the bean sprouts, then drain well.

3 Roughly chop the mint. Combine the ingredients from **A** together and mix well.

4 Arrange the mackerel, onion, bean sprouts, mint and peanut dressing on a plate. Sprinkle with more red chili pepper flakes, to taste. Mix well before eating.

Korean White Fish Carpaccio **Hoe Deopbap**

Aromatic herbs and vegetables simply flavored with salt and sesame, are wrapped in or mixed with thin slices of fresh raw white fish in this classic Korean dish. It's great served on top of warm steamed rice too.

SERVES 2
PREP TIME: 30 MINUTES

7 oz (200 g) sashimi-grade boneless, skinless white fish such as sea bream or flounder

One 4-inch (10-cm) piece leek (the white part)

One 1-inch (2.5-cm) piece fresh ginger, peeled and minced

2 teaspoons roasted white sesame seeds, divided

3 Korean perilla leaves

⅔ teaspoon salt

2 teaspoons sesame oil, divided

DIRECTIONS

1 Cut the fish at a 45° angle into very thin slices.

2 Cut into the leek lengthwise and remove the core. Shred into long thin strips. Put the ginger and leek into separate bowls of cold water and soak for 5 minutes (see photo a). Drain well.

3 Coarsely grind the sesame seeds with a mortar and pestle (see photo b).

4 Tear the perilla leaves into bite-size pieces and put them into a bowl. Add the leek, ginger, salt, ⅔ of roasted sesame seeds and 1 teaspoon of sesame oil (see photo c), and mix to coat the vegetables in the sesame oil and seeds.

5 Arrange the fish slices on a plate. Top with the combined vegetables from Step **4**, and sprinkle with the remaining sesame seeds and sesame oil.

This is also delicious dipped into the Korean Gochujang Dressing described on page 15. The dressing is very rich, so it's great eaten with plain rice or as an appetizer with drinks.

a

b

c

TIP *Hoe refers to several Korean dishes made with raw ingredients; hoe deopbap is made with white fish. It is commonly eaten with gochujang and kimchi and wrapped in red leaf lettuce or Korean perilla leaves. In this recipe, the white fish is topped with herbs dressed with salt and sesame oil. If you don't have perilla leaves, you can also use Japanese green shiso leaves. This dish features nutty roasted white sesame seeds, which are used quite often in Korean cuisine. Although it's a bit of a chore to grind the sesame seeds, the results are well worth it!*

Clam, Dill and Fried Omelette Salad

This pan-fried Vietnamese omelette with steamed clam juice and dill is amazingly delicious.

SERVES 2
PREP TIME: 15 MINUTES
COOKING TIME: 5 MINUTES

7 oz (200 g) Manila clams or small littleneck clams, de-sanded
2 tablespoons sesame oil, divided
1 clove garlic, peeled and finely minced
2 tablespoons sake
3 large eggs
2 stalks dill, roughly chopped, plus additional dill for topping (optional)

DIRECTIONS

1 Rinse the clams well while rubbing the shells together. Drain. Put 1 teaspoon of the sesame oil in a pan over medium heat. Add the garlic, and when the oil becomes fragrant, add in the clams and stir-fry quickly. Add the sake, and cover the pan with a lid. Steam-cook the claims for around 2½ minutes, until the clam shells open. Discard any unopened clams.

2 Break the eggs into a bowl, and add 2 tablespoons of the clam steaming liquid and the dill. Whisk well.

3 Heat the remaining 1 teaspoon of the sesame oil in a pan over medium heat. Pour in the egg mixture. Pan-fry the omelette while stirring with cooking chopsticks or a fork until it's about 70% set.

4 Arrange the omelette on a serving plate with the clams. Optionally sprinkle with additional chopped dill.

Stir-fried Celery and Crabmeat with Shaoxing Wine

This salad-like stir-fry, or stir-fried salad, combines the delicious flavor of fresh crabmeat with the crunchiness of celery and the sweetness of leek. It is a great dish to eat with plain steamed rice.

SERVES 2
PREP TIME: 10 MINUTES
COOKING TIME: 5 MINUTES

1 celery stalk
5 celery leaves
½ leek (the white part)
2 teaspoons sesame oil
One 1-inch (2.5-cm) piece fresh ginger, peeled and finely diced
4 oz (100 g) fresh crabmeat

A
┌ 1 tablespoon Shaoxing wine (or sake)
└ ¼ teaspoon salt

DIRECTIONS

1 Remove the tough outer strings from the celery stalk and thinly slice diagonally. Shred the celery leaves finely. Thinly slice the leek diagonally.

2 Heat the sesame oil and ginger in a pan over medium heat. When the oil is fragrant, add the vegetables from Step 1 and the crab meat. Stir-fry briefly. Add the **A** ingredients, and continue to stir-fry until the vegetables are crisp-tender.

Jellyfish and Cucumber Salad

This is a great salad to have on a hot summer's day. It's also a great appetizer to serve with white or sparkling wine!

SERVES 2
PREP TIME: 20 MINUTES

1 ⅓ oz (40 g) salted jellyfish
1 small cucumber
¼ teaspoon salt
A ⌈ 1 tablespoon fresh lemon juice
  ⌊ 1 tablespoon *nuoc mam*
½ cup (10 g) fresh mint leaves, loosely packed
1 tablespoon sesame oil

DIRECTIONS

1 Rinse the jellyfish briefly, and soak in water for 15 minutes to remove the salt. Drain well and cut into easy-to-eat strips.

2 Cut the cucumber diagonally into ¼ inch (5 mm) wide slices. Sprinkle with the salt, and rub it into the cucumber until it is wilted. Squeeze firmly to eliminate excess moisture.

3 Combine the ingredients in **A** in a bowl. Add the ingredients from Steps **1** and **2** and the mint leaves into the bowl, and toss well. Drizzle in the sesame oil, and mix lightly.

TIP Although salted jellyfish is known as a Chinese ingredient, Vietnam also has mixed jellyfish dishes called *goi sua*. Here, I boosted the Vietnamese flavors by adding fresh mint. The lemon juice adds a refreshing acidity, and the sesame oil adds richness to this dish. You can find salted jellyfish at general Asian or Chinese grocery stores.

Lotus Root and Shrimp with Vietnamese Dressing

The textures of the plump, tender shrimp and the crunchy lotus root work together so well. This dish looks as good as it tastes, so it's a nice item to serve to guests.

SERVES 2
PREP TIME: 15 MINUTES
COOKING TIME: 15 MINUTES

5 oz (150 g) lotus root
8 large shrimp (such as black tiger)
2 tablespoons potato starch or cornstarch
2 tablespoons sake, divided
3 tablespoons Vietnamese Nuoc Mam Dressing (see page 15)
1 teaspoon sesame oil

DIRECTIONS

1 Peel the lotus root, slice in half lengthwise, and slice into ⅛ inch (3 mm) thick half moons. Put into a bowl of cold water and soak for 3 minutes.

2 De-vein the shrimp and sprinkle with the potato starch or cornstarch Rub it in well, and then rinse off. (This cleans the shrimp.)

3 Bring a pan of water to a boil and add 1 tablespoon of the sake. Boil the lotus root slices for 90 seconds. Take the lotus root out (keep the water for the next step), drain well and pat dry with paper towels.

4 Add the remaining 1 tablespoon of the sake to the boiling water from Step **3**. Boil the shrimp in the water for about 90 seconds. Turn off the heat, cover with a lid, and leave the shrimp until cooked through in the residual heat. Drain the shrimp, pat dry and peel.

5 Put the lotus root and shrimp in a bowl with the dressing and toss to coat. Drizzle in the sesame oil and mix briefly.

TIP *The lotus flower is the national flower of Vietnam, and the lotus root is commonly seen in Vietnamese cuisine. It is paired with shrimp, which is also frequently used in Vietnamese cuisine, and flavored with the nuoc-mam-based coriander dressing, making for a thoroughly Vietnamese-inspired salad. Shrimp can become hard when overcooked, so be sure to cook with the residual heat to keep it tender.*

Chapter 4
Salads with Meat and Chicken

Salads that combine beef, pork or chicken with fresh herbs and vegetables are popular in many Asian cuisines. These salads work especially well as main dish salads, or served on top of rice (see pages 12–13) to make a complete meal in a bowl.

Crispy Pork and Watercress Salad (photo on facing page)

The lemongrass-scented fried pork belly tastes surprisingly light. The coriander-flavored dressing and watercress make this a very refreshing salad.

SERVES 2
PREP TIME: 10 MINUTES
COOKING TIME: 15 MINUTES

⅓ red onion
1⅔ oz (50 g) watercress
5½ oz (165 g) sliced pork belly (8 slices, about ¼ inch / 5 mm thick)
2 tablespoons flour
2 stalks lemongrass, each about 7 inches (18 cm) long
2 teaspoons sesame oil
2 tablespoons Vietnamese Nuoc Mam Dressing (page 15)
2 or 3 lemon wedges, for serving

DIRECTIONS

1 Thinly slice the onion thinly lengthwise. Soak in water for 3 minutes, and then drain well. Roughly chop the watercress and mix together with the onion.
2 Dust the pork with flour. Twist the lemongrass to tenderize it. Heat the sesame oil in a pan over medium heat, and pan-fry the pork and lemongrass until the pork is crispy.
3 Put the pork and lemongrass in a bowl with the dressing and mix to coat. Add the onion and water cress and toss briefly. Serve with the lemon.

Spicy Coconut Chicken with Lemongrass and Coriander

These flavors are unlike any you have experienced, with the taste of lemongrass and the aroma of coconut milk.

SERVES 2
PREP TIME: 10 MINUTES
COOKING TIME: 15 MINUTES

12 oz (350 g) chicken breast meat
2 stalks lemongrass stems, each about 8 inches (20 cm) long
6 fresh coriander stalks, plus more for garnish
1 tablespoon olive oil
A ⌈ 4 tablespoons coconut milk
    │ 1 clove garlic, peeled and grated
    │ One 1-inch (2.5-cm) piece fresh ginger, peeled and grated
    │ ½ raw red chili pepper, thinly sliced with seeds removed
    └ 1 tablespoon white wine
1 tablespoon *nam pla*
1 egg, beaten

DIRECTIONS

1 Cut the chicken at a 45° angle into ½-inch (1.5-cm) widths. Cut the lemongrass in half lengthwise, and into lengths of 1½ inches (4 cm). Roughly chop the coriander.
2 Heat the oil in a pan over medium heat, and stir-fry the chicken. When the chicken browns, mix the ingredients in **A**, and add them with the lemongrass into the pan. Once it starts to boil, reduce to low heat and simmer for 5 minutes.
3 Add in the *nam pla* and mix to coat. Drizzle in the egg. When the egg is half cooked, quickly stir everything together, and serve on a plate. Garnish with coriander.

Chicken and Shrimp Glass Noodle Salad Yum Woon Sen

Packed with chicken, shrimp and coriander, this hearty glass noodle salad is a great side dish with plain rice. The glass noodles absorb lots of flavor and become really tasty on their own.

SERVES 2
PREP TIME: 30 MINUTES
COOKING TIME: 15 MINUTES

6 large shrimp (such as black tiger shrimp)
2 tablespoons potato starch or corn-starch
1 tablespoon sake
2 teaspoons sesame oil
4 oz (100 g) ground chicken
3 tablespoons Thai Nam Pla Dressing (see page 15), divided
2 oz (50 g) glass or cellophane noodles
2 dried wood ear mushrooms
½ red onion
6 fresh coriander stalks

DIRECTIONS

1 De-vein the shrimp, sprinkle with potato starch or cornstarch, and rub it in. Rinse off the starch. (This cleans the shrimp.) Bring a pan of water to a boil, add the sake and boil the shrimp for 90 seconds. Turn off the heat, cover the pan and leave the shrimp to cook in residual heat (see photo a). When they are cooked through, drain and pat dry.

2 Heat the sesame oil in a pan over medium heat. Stir-fry the ground chicken until it changes color. Add 2 tablespoons of the dressing (see photo b), and continue to stir-fry until there is no moisture left in the pan.

3 Cook the glass noodles in boiling water for two minutes, and then drain into a colander. Pat dry with paper towels (see photo c), and then cut into easy-to-eat lengths.

4 Soak the wood ear mushroom in warm water for 15 minutes. Remove the tough stems. Cook them in boiling water for 2 minutes, and then drain well and slice thinly.

5 Slice the onion thinly, place the slices into a bowl of cold water for 3 minutes, and then drain and pat them dry. Roughly chop the coriander.

6 Peel the shrimp and cut them into ¾ inch (2 cm) long pieces. Put all the ingredients into a bowl, add the remaining tablespoon of dressing and toss well to coat.

This dish is delicious as it is, but you can wrap it in some leafy vegetables such as lettuce for more of a salad texture!

a

b

c

TIP Thai cuisine is increasingly popular. In Thai, *yum* means to dress, and *woon sen* refers to glass noodles. You can modify this recipe as you please, substituting squid for shrimp or chicken breast for ground chicken. The cooked glass noodles are the stars of the show. Properly removing the moisture by patting the noodles dry in a paper towel is an integral step.

Chicken Salad with Chrysanthemum Greens & Peanuts

The chicken in this delicious salad is steamed in an aromatic mix of lemongrass, kaffir lime leaves and ginger, which gives it a refreshing taste and makes it very tender and juicy too.

SERVES 2
PREP TIME: 15 MINUTES
COOKING TIME: 15 MINUTES

3½ oz (100 g) chrysanthemum greens (or Swiss chard)

4 green onions (scallions)

2 tablespoons whole unsalted peanuts

10 oz (330 g) boneless skinless chicken thigh

A
- Two 8-inch (20-cm) pieces lemongrass stalk (the root ends), cut in half lengthwise
- 1 kaffir lime leaf
- One 1-inch (2.5-cm) piece fresh ginger, peeled and minced
- 2 tablespoons sake
- 1 tablespoon sesame oil

1 tablespoon *nam pla*

1 tablespoon fresh lemon juice

DIRECTIONS

1 Remove the tough stem ends of the chrysanthemum greens and cut them into 1½-inch (4-cm) pieces. Cut the green onion into 1½-inch (4-cm) pieces. Roughly chop up the peanuts.

2 Butterfly the chicken by making an incision into the thick part horizontally and opening the meat out. Pound the chicken lightly with the side of a heavy kitchen knife to make it a uniform thickness.

3 Put the chicken into a frying pan. Add the **A** ingredients and turn on the heat to medium. Bring the sake to a boil, turn the heat down to low, cover the pan and steam-cook for about 7 minutes. Turn off the heat and leave the pan to cool down for a few minutes. Take out the chicken and slice into bite-size pieces.

4 Add the *nam pla* to the liquid remaining in the frying pan in Step **3**, and bring to a boil over medium heat. Turn off the heat and add the lemon juice.

5 Put the ingredients from Steps **1** and **3** into a bowl, add the mixture from Step **4** and mix together quickly.

Chicken & Green Onions with Spicy Sesame Dressing

With a rich, sesame-packed dressing with the bite of Szechuan pepper and juicy, flavorful steamed chicken, this salad is simply delicious!

SERVES 2 TO 3
PREP TIME: 10 MINUTES
COOKING TIME: 20 MINUTES

10 oz (330 g) boneless skinless chicken thigh

A
- **1 teaspoon ground Szechuan pepper**
- **2 tablespoons Shaoxing wine (or sake)**
- **1 tablespoon sesame oil**

4 thin green onions (scallions)

8 oz (250 g) bean sprouts

B
- **3 tablespoons sesame paste (or tahini)**
- **1 clove garlic, peeled and finely chopped**
- **One 4-inch (10-cm) piece leek (the white part)**
- **½ teaspoon coarsely ground chili pepper**
- **1 tablespoon soy sauce**

DIRECTIONS

1 Place the chicken on a heat-resistant dish and add the ingredients from **A** to it. Place the dish with the chicken in a steamer, and steam over high heat for about 10 minutes. Reserve the steaming water.

2 Chop the green onions finely. Remove the thin roots from the bean sprouts and place them in a colander. Pour boiling water over the sprouts, and drain well.

3 Put the ingredients in **B** and ⅓ cup of the reserved steaming water from Step **1** in a bowl and mix to combine.

4 Cut the steamed chicken into bite-size pieces and arrange on a serving plate. Top with the green onions and bean sprouts, and drizzle on the dressing made in Step **3**.

Oven-baked Tandoori Chicken Salad

This dish is so easy to make yet it looks really festive, and is perfect for serving to guests. Not only is the spice-marinated chicken packed with flavor, the vegetables really stand out too.

SERVES 2 TO 3
PREP TIME: 20 MINUTES
COOKING TIME: 12 MINUTES

10 oz (330 g) boneless chicken breast

A
- 3 tablespoons plain unsweetened yogurt
- 1 clove garlic, peeled and grated
- One 1-inch (2.5-cm) piece fresh ginger, peeled and grated
- ½ teaspoon coriander powder
- 1 teaspoon ground cumin
- 1 teaspoon salt
- 2 tablespoons dry white wine

½ white onion
2 small green bell peppers
4 to 6 cherry tomatoes
2 tablespoons olive oil
Ground cumin, to taste (optional)

DIRECTIONS

1 Optionally remove the skin from the chicken breast, cut into bite-size pieces and place in a bowl. Add the ingredients from **A** and rub them into the chicken. Allow to rest for 15 minutes while the flavors penetrate the meat.

2 Cut the onion into 3 wedges. Cut the green bell peppers in half lengthwise and remove the seeds.

3 Preheat the oven to 430°F (220°C). Put the chicken, onion, green peppers and tomatoes on a baking tray and drizzle with the olive oil. Bake for about 12 minutes. Transfer to a serving plate, and optionally sprinkle with more ground cumin, to taste.

TIP This recipe combines chicken marinated in a tandoori-chicken-style marinade with vegetables that are baked with the chicken to make a warm salad. Although the vegetables are not seasoned separately, they absorb the flavors of the marinade, which enhances the natural sweetness of the vegetables without drowning them out. Try using other vegetables for this such as cabbage or eggplant.

Crispy Vietnamese Pancakes **Bánh Xéo**

Combine the stir-fried pork and fresh vegetables with the dressing and stuff them into the pancake just before eating.

MAKES TWO 8-IN (20-CM) DIAMETER PANCAKES
PREP TIME: 15 MINUTES
COOKING TIME: 20 MINUTES

A
- 4 tablespoons cake flour
- 2 tablespoons coconut milk
- 2 tablespoons water
- ½ teaspoon turmeric

1 medium egg
4 oz (100 g) boneless pork leg
4 oz (100 g) bean sprouts
Salt, to taste
1 teaspoon sesame oil, plus more for frying
½ red onion
½ red bell pepper
Coriander and mint, to taste

B
- ½ fresh red chili pepper, chopped
- ½ teaspoon white sugar
- 1 tablespoon *nuoc mam*
- ½ tablespoon vinegar
- 2 teaspoons water

DIRECTIONS

1 Combine the ingredients in **A** in a bowl, and whisk until smooth. Break in the egg and mix thoroughly.

2 Slice the pork into strips, and remove the thin roots from the bean sprouts.

3 Heat some sesame oil in a frying pan over medium heat, and stir-fry the pork. When it's cooked through, add the bean sprouts, season with salt and stir-fry briefly. Remove from the frying pan.

4 Wipe out the frying pan with paper towels, add 1 teaspoon of the sesame oil and heat over medium heat. Pour in half of the batter from Step **1** and tilt the pan to spread the batter to the edges.

5 When the pancake is cooked about two thirds of the way, place half of the ingredients from Step **3** on top. Fold the pancake in half. When the bottom is crispy, transfer to a serving plate. Prepare the other pancake in the same way.

6 Thinly slice the red onion and red bell pepper lengthwise. Roughly chop the coriander. Arrange these on the plates along with the pancakes Combine the dressing ingredients in **B** and serve separately on the side.

....

TIP *Banh xeo is a popular Vietnamese dish consisting of very crispy pancakes made with coconut milk and turmeric filled with vegetables and meat. It typically combines pork with crispy bean sprouts for the filling and mixes them with a mountain of fresh herbs.*

Thai Crispy Pork Salad   Yum Moo Yang

Flavorful pork belly, refreshing lemon and spicy onions go together so well! This salad is great as a side dish with rice, or as a drinking appetizer!

SERVES 2
PREP TIME: 10 MINUTES
COOKING TIME: 10 MINUTES

½ **medium white onion**

1 **red bell pepper**

Sesame oil for frying

1 **clove garlic, peeled and thinly sliced**

7 oz (200 g) **thin pork belly slices**

A
- 2 **lemon slices cut into quarters**
- 2 **tablespoons fresh lemon juice**
- 1 **tablespoon** *nam pla*

⅓ cup (7 g) **mint leaves, loosely packed**

8 **Thai or holy basil leaves**

Coarsely ground black pepper, to taste

DIRECTIONS

1 Finely chop the onion and put it into a bowl of cold water. Soak for 5 minutes, and then drain well.

2 Slice the red bell pepper thinly crosswise.

3 Heat some sesame oil and the garlic in a pan over medium heat. When the oil is fragrant, add the pork. Fry the pork, turning occasionally and wiping out any excess fat and moisture from the pan with a wadded up paper towel until the pork is crispy.

4 Combine the onion from Step **1** and the ingredients in **A** in a bowl. Add the ingredients from Step **3** and mix. Transfer to serving plates, add the bell pepper, mint and basil, and sprinkle with black pepper.

> TIP In Thai, *yum* means "to mix," *moo* means "pork", and *yang* means "to cook with dry heat," so *yum moo yang* refers to a mixed vegetable and grilled pork salad. Here, I've pan-fried the pork instead of grilling it and combined it with *nam pla*, lemon, and onion. The keys to this dish are to wipe out the excess fat that comes out of the pork as it cooks, and to drain the moisture from the onion thoroughly.

Thai Beef Salad Yum Nua Yang

The refreshing herbs and vegetables enhance the delicious flavor of the beef. The spicy bite of red chili pepper and the crunch of the peanuts add just the right accents.

SERVES 2
PREP TIME: 15 MINUTES
COOKING TIME: 5 MINUTES

½ **red onion**
1 **small cucumber**
1 **fresh red chili pepper**
4 **lemongrass leaves, each around 8**
    inches (20 cm) long
2 **teaspoons sesame oil**
7 **oz (200 g) thinly sliced beef (about ¼**
    inch / 5 mm thick)
3 **tablespoons Thai Nam Pla Dressing**
    (see page 15)
12 **to 15 Thai or holy basil leaves**
2 **tablespoons whole unsalted peanuts,**
    roughly chopped

DIRECTIONS

1 Thinly slice the red onion. Soak the slices in a bowl of cold water for 3 minutes and drain thoroughly.

2 Cut the cucumber in half lengthwise and remove the seeds. Thinly slice the cucumber diagonally. Finely chop the red chili pepper.

3 Cut the lemongrass into 2–3 pieces each. Heat the sesame oil in a pan over medium heat, and sauté the beef, turning once. When the beef is browned, add the lemongrass and dressing. Mix briefly to coat the beef with the dressing.

4 Transfer the beef to serving plates. Combine the onion and bell pepper, and arrange on the plates with the basil. Sprinkle with the chopped peanuts.

....

TIP This salad features *nua yang*, beef cooked over dry heat. It's often grilled but here I have simply pan-fried it. In this recipe, which I developed based on the memory of a dish I had at a Thai restaurant once, the beef is combined with vegetables and fresh herbs. The pan-fried beef is combined with lemongrass and *nam-pla*-based dressing to add freshness and flavor. You can use beef offcuts for this recipe.

Korean Beef Tongue and Green Onion Salad

The beef tongue, which has more flavor the more you chew it, and the slight bitterness of the chrysanthemum greens are brought together by the black vinegar dressing in this hearty main dish salad.

SERVES 2
PREP TIME: 10 MINUTES
COOKING TIME: 10 MINUTES

4 green onions (scallions)

2 oz (50 g) chrysanthemum greens (or Swiss chard)

2 teaspoons sesame oil

7 oz (200 g) sliced beef tongue (available at Korean grocery stores)

A
- **1 teaspoon white sugar**
- **2 tablespoons black vinegar**
- **1 tablespoon soy sauce**

2 tablespoons pine nuts

1 teaspoon coarsely ground red chili pepper

DIRECTIONS

1 Finely chop the green onions. Remove the tough stems from the chrysanthemum greens, and cut the leaves into 1 ½ inch (4 cm) long pieces.

2 Heat the sesame oil in a frying pan over medium heat. Add the beef tongue and sauté for about 2 minutes, turning it when it changes color.

3 Combine the ingredients from **A** in a bowl. Add the pine nuts and ingredients from Steps **1** and **2**, and mix to coat the ingredients evenly. Sprinkle with the coarsely ground red chili pepper.

TIP When I visited South Korea, I discovered that people eat grilled meat with lots of vegetables there. This healthy way of eating changed my preconceptions about Korean barbecue, which I'd thought was very meat-heavy. In this recipe I've combined the elements of a grilled meat meal into a salad, using pine nuts, which are used often in Korean cuisine, as an accent. Try using loose leaf lettuce or Korean perilla leaves to make this taste even more authentically Korean.

Spicy Korean Salad with Boiled Pork and Perilla

The pork in this recipe is simmered slowly so that all the fat is rendered out, leaving the meat tender and moist. Combined with the spicy dressing, it's so delicious. The unique flavor of the perilla adds a distinct accent.

SERVES 2 TO 3
PREP TIME: 15 MINUTES
COOKING TIME: 90 MINUTES

14 oz (400 g) pork loin

⅓ teaspoon salt

A ⌈ **One 1-inch (2.5-cm) piece fresh ginger, peeled and shredded**
  ⌊ **2 tablespoons sake**

4 loose leaf lettuce leaves

4 Korean perilla leaves

2 tablespoons Korean Gochujang Dressing (see page 15)

Ground white sesame seeds, to taste

DIRECTIONS

1 Bring the pork to room temperature. Rub the salt into the meat.

2 Bring a pan of water (enough to cover the pork) to a boil and add the ingredients from **A**. Put the pork in the boiling water, and bring back to a boil. Turn the heat down to low, and simmer the pork for about an hour while skimming off any scum. Turn off the heat and leave the pork to cool in the water until it can be handled. Slice into ⅓ inch (1 cm) thick slices.

3 Tear the lettuce and Korean perilla leaves into easy-to-eat pieces.

4 Put the ingredients from Steps **2** and **3** into a bowl. Swirl in the dressing, and toss to coat. Transfer to serving plates, and sprinkle with ground sesame seeds, to taste.

....

TIP I based this salad on a popular Korean pork dish called *bossam*. The salad is dressed with a mixture of typical Korean ingredients including *gochujang*, red chili pepper and sesame seeds, and goes well with white rice. The keys to making the delicious boiled pork are to rub the salt very thoroughly into the meat and to simmer it gently at a low heat.

Spicy Salad with Pork, Mint Leaves and Red Cabbage

This is a very refreshing salad with a spicy-hot bite. The red cabbage mellows out the flavors.

SERVES 2
PREP TIME: 15 MINUTES
COOKING TIME: 10 MINUTES

7 oz (200 g) thinly sliced lean pork

1 cup (20 g) mint leaves, loosely packed

4 coriander stalks

2 kaffir lime leaves (optional)

2 teaspoons sesame oil

A ⎡ 2 tablespoons Thai Nam Pla Dressing (see page 15)
  ⎣ 2 tablespoons sake

½ teaspoon coarsely ground red chili pepper

½ lime

¼ head medium red cabbage, sliced

Additional coarsely ground red chili pepper, to taste

DIRECTIONS

1 Slice the pork into ⅓ inch (1 cm) wide strips.

2 Roughly chop the mint and coriander, and finely shred the kaffir lime leaves, if using.

3 Heat the sesame oil in the frying pan over medium heat and stir fry the pork from Step **1**. Once the pork changes color, add the ingredients from **A**. Stir-fry until the moisture is gone.

4 Put the coarsely ground red chili pepper and the ingredients from Steps **2** and **3** into a bowl. Squeeze the lime into the bowl and toss to evenly coat the ingredients. Arrange on a plate with the shredded red cabbage. Sprinkle with additional coarsely ground red chili pepper, to taste.

TIP *This is my take on a Thai pork salad called larb mu. After seasoning the pork well, combine it with herbs for a refreshing flavor.*

Beef and Avocado Thai Salad

The *nam pla* and lemon juice permeate the beef, making it so delicious. Avocado lovers won't be able to resist this dish.

SERVES 2
PREP TIME: 15 MINUTES
COOKING TIME: 10 MINUTES

A {
- ½ fresh red chili pepper, de-seeded
- 1 tablespoon fresh lemon juice
- 1 tablespoon *nam pla*

- 1 tablespoon sake
- 7 oz (200 g) thinly sliced beef
- 1 avocado
- 1 tablespoon fresh lemon juice
- ⅓ red onion
- 4 coriander stalks
- 3 green onions (scallions)
- 1 tablespoon sesame oil

DIRECTIONS

1 Combine the ingredients from **A** in a bowl.

2 Bring a pan of water to a boil and add the sake. Add beef to the boiling water one slice at a time, cooking each slice for about 40 seconds then taking it out immediately. Put the beef into the bowl from Step **1** while it's still warm, and mix to coat it with the dressing.

3 Cut the avocado in half, remove the stone and peel it. Cut the avocado into 1-inch (2.5-cm) pieces, and drizzle the lemon juice over them.

4 Slice the red onion thinly, and soak the slices in a bowl of cold water for 3 minutes. Drain well. Roughly chop the coriander, and cut the green onions into ¾ inch (2 cm) long pieces.

5 Add the ingredients from Steps **3** and **4** to the bowl. Swirl in the sesame oil and toss briefly to coat all the ingredients.

| TIP | This is my version of a Thai salad that combines boiled beef and vegetables with a *nam-pla*-based dressing. I added avocado to make this a very hearty salad. |

Chapter 5
Salads with Fritters, Spring Rolls and Other Fried Snacks

This chapter has recipes for what I call "fried salads," delicious fried items from around Asia such as fish cakes from Vietnam, spring rolls from Thailand and China, and samosas from India, that are combined with lots of fresh vegetables and herbs. All these salads are hearty and filling, perfect as a main side dish with rice or a one-dish meal. Your family will love them!

Fish Fritter Salad (photo on facing page)

This is a flavorful, spicy salad. The fish nuggets are coated in a beer batter, which makes them very light and crispy.

SERVES 2
PREP TIME: 20 MINUTES
COOKING TIME: 10 MINUTES

14 oz (400 g) firm white fish fillets (such as cod or sea bass)
Salt, for sprinkling the fish
4 coriander stalks
4 green onions (scallions)
1 egg, beaten
3 tablespoons cake flour, divided
Scant ½ cup (100 ml) lager beer
Oil for deep frying
2 tablespoons Thai Nam Pla Dressing (see page 15)
½ teaspoon coarsely ground red chili pepper, plus more, to taste

DIRECTIONS

1 Sprinkle the fish with salt and leave for 10 minutes. Pat dry with paper towels, and cut into bite-size pieces.
2 Cut the coriander and green onions into 2-in (5-cm) pieces.
3 Combine the beaten egg, 1 tablespoon of the cake flour and beer to make the batter.
4 Dust the fish with the remaining 2 tablespoons of cake flour and dip it into the batter. Fill a pan with about ¾ inch (2 cm) of oil. Heat the oil to 355°F (180°C). Fry the fish for about 4 minutes until golden brown, turning occasionally.
5 Combine the dressing and ½ teaspoon chili pepper in a bowl. Add the ingredients from Step **2** and toss quickly. Serve on a plate with additional chili pepper, to taste.

Fried Green Banana Salad with Thai Basil

Fried green bananas are popular at food stalls and other eateries in Thailand, and are so addictive! You can substitute unripe regular bananas.

SERVES 2 TO 3
PREP TIME: 10 MINUTES
COOKING TIME: 10 MINUTES

4 green bananas
Cake flour, as needed
Oil for deep frying
1 clove garlic, thinly sliced
A ⌈ 2 tablespoons fresh lemon juice
  ⌊ 1 tablespoon *nam pla*
12 Thai or holy basil leaves, torn
2 tablespoons fried onion flakes (available at Asian grocery stores)

DIRECTIONS

1 Cut the green banana into ¾-inch (2-cm) pieces. Dust the banana pieces with flour.
2 Heat the oil to 355°F (180°C) and put in the garlic. Fry until crispy, then remove from the oil. Put the bananas into the oil and fry for around 2 minutes until they just start to change color, turning them occasionally.
3 Arrange the bananas on a plate. Combine the **A** ingredients and pour over the bananas. Add the basil and toss to combine. Sprinkle with the fried garlic from Step **2** and the fried onion.

Vietnamese-style Fried Fish Cake and Herb Salad

These homemade deep-fried fish cakes are amazingly good! Combined with the refreshing taste of herbs, this is a salad you'll want to have with a cold beer.

SERVES 2 TO 3
PREP TIME: 20 MINUTES
COOKING TIME: 10 MINUTES

7 oz (200 g) white fish fillets (such as sea bream or Spanish mackerel)

A {
1 oz (30 g) *shirasuboshi* or salted semi-dried whitebait (available at Japanese grocery stores, or substitute 2 drained canned anchovy fillets)
¼ leek (the white part), minced
One 3-inch (7.5-cm) piece fresh ginger, peeled and roughly chopped
1 tablespoon potato starch or cornstarch
1 egg white
1 pinch salt
}

Sesame oil, as needed
4 oz (100 g) bean sprouts
10 Thai or holy basil leaves
Scant ½ cup (8 g) mint leaves, loosely packed
1 lime wedge
½ fresh red chili pepper, de-seeded
2 tablespoons *nuoc mam*
1 tablespoon fresh lime juice

DIRECTIONS

1 Skin the fish, remove any bones, and roughly cut up.

2 Put the fish and the ingredients in **A** into a food processor (see photo a), and blend until smooth. Divide the paste into quarters, and shape each quarter into an oval patty (see photo b).

3 Fill a pan with about ¾ inch (2 cm) of sesame oil, and heat it to 340°F (170°C). Put in the patties from Step **2** into the pan and deep-fry for about 4 minutes until a light golden brown, turning occasionally (see photo c).

4 Remove the thin roots from the bean sprouts and place them in a colander. Pour boiling water over them, and drain well.

5 Slice the fish cakes into easy-to-eat pieces and arrange on a plate along with the bean sprouts, basil and mint. Cut the lime wedge in half and place on the plate. Combine the chili pepper, *nuoc mam* and lime juice, and drizzle over all.

Serve these fish cakes while they're piping hot. In Vietnam, they're usually oval shaped, as pictured above.

a

b

c

TIP Deep-fried fish cakes are called *cha ca* in Vietnamese. There are many ways *cha ca* is enjoyed in Vietnam, such as putting them in a banh mi sandwich or on pho noodles. Here, I've combined them with vegetables and herbs to make a salad. If you add salted fish (such as the *shirasuboshi* used here) in addition to the fish fillets, the flavor becomes deeper and more complex.

Loose Leaf Lettuce Salad with Vegetarian Samosas

The garlic-flavored yogurt dressing and the samosas complement each other perfectly! The final sprinkle of parsley is essential, as it ties together all of the flavors in this dish.

SERVES 2 TO 3
PREP TIME: 30 MINUTES
COOKING TIME: 30 MINUTES

2 medium potatoes

⅓ white onion

2 oz (50 g) shelled green peas

A
- 1 clove garlic, peeled and grated
- ⅓ teaspoon salt
- ⅓ teaspoon coriander powder
- ½ teaspoon cumin powder
- ¼ teaspoon *garam masala*

8 gyoza dumpling skins (also called potsticker wrappers; available at Chinese or Japanese grocery stores)

Olive oil for frying

5 loose leaf lettuce leaves

3 to 4 tablespoons Indian Yogurt Dressing (see page 15)

1 tablespoon minced parsley

DIRECTIONS

1 Fill a steamer (or the pan underneath a steamer basket) with water and bring to a boil. Put the potatoes in the steamer, and steam for 20 minutes over high heat. Peel the potatoes while they're still hot and mash them with a fork or masher.

2 Finely mince the onion and put it in a heat-resistant dish. Cover with plastic wrap and microwave for about 2 minutes. Add the onions, the green peas, and the ingredients in **A** to the potatoes from Step **1**. Mix well to combine.

3 Divide the mixture from Step **2** into eight equal portions. Place each portion on a gyoza dumpling wrapper and moisten the edges of the wrapper with water (see photo a). Wrap the wrapper around the filling and bring the edges together in a triangular shape to form the samosas (see photo b).

4 Fill a frying pan with ¾ inch (2 cm) of olive oil, and heat the oil to 355°F (180°C). Put in the samosas and pan-fry them until golden brown, about 2 minutes, turning occasionally (see photo c).

5 Tear the lettuce into easy-to-eat pieces. Toss together quickly with the samosas and arrange on a serving plate. Pour on the dressing, and sprinkle with parsley.

The peas add a beautiful green accent. Coat the samosas in the dressing and enjoy with the crisp lettuce leaves!

a

b

c

TIP *Samosas are very popular in Indian homes. When I traveled to India, I often caught glimpses of children munching on these delicious morsels as snacks. You can add a variety of ingredients to the filling such as ground meat or beans. Here, I've kept the samosas simple, and served them with leafy greens such as lettuce to make a hearty salad.*

Fried Spring Rolls with Fresh Herbs

These rice-paper wrapped spring rolls have a lovely light, crispy texture. When they are combined with the fresh tastes of coriander and mint, I feel like I could keep eating them forever.

SERVES 2 TO 3
PREP TIME: 40 MINUTES
COOKING TIME: 15 MINUTES

1 oz (30 g) glass or cellophane noodles
5 oz (150 g) ground pork

A
- **One 6-inch (15-cm) piece leek (the white part), finely chopped**
- **½ beaten egg**
- **1 tablespoon Thai Nam Pla Dressing (see page 15)**
- **1 tablespoon sake**

8 rice paper wrappers
Olive oil for frying
4 oz (100 g) bean sprouts

B
- **4 coriander stalks, roughly chopped**
- **Scant ½ cup (8 g) mint leaves, roughly chopped**
- **1 lime, cut into 8 wedges**

2 tablespoons Thai Nam Pla Dressing (see page 15)
½ fresh red chili pepper, de-seeded and finely chopped

DIRECTIONS

1 Soak the glass noodles in lukewarm water for 5 minutes until softened, and drain well. Cut the noodles into ⅓-inch (1-cm) pieces, and put them in a bowl with the ground pork and ingredients in **A**. Mix well until it the meat becomes sticky to make the filling.

2 Divide the filling into eight portions. Put a rice paper wrapper on a piece of wax paper, and spray the surface with water until it becomes soft and pliable. Place a portion of the filling on the edge of the wrapper closest to you. Roll up the wrapper once, fold in the sides and finish rolling it up. Repeat with the remaining wrappers and filling.

3 Fill a frying pan with ¾ inch (2 cm) of olive oil, and heat the oil to 355°F (180°C). Put in the spring rolls and fry them for about 6 minutes until light golden brown and crispy, turning occasionally. Drain.

4 Remove the thin roots from the bean sprouts, put them in a colander and pour boiling water over them. Drain well.

5 Arrange the spring rolls and bean sprouts on a serving plate, along with the ingredients in **B**. Combine the Thai Nam Pla Dressing and the chili pepper and serve it on the side.

TIP Called *popia thot* in Thai, deep-fried spring rolls are one of the most popular dishes in Thai cuisine. They are delicious with hot or sweet chili sauce, but try them with my original dressing too. Rice paper wrappers can be hard to handle if they get too wet, so the trick is to just moisten them with a spray bottle.

Fried Fish Nuggets with Carrot and Onion Chili Sauce

This is my version of a fried fish dish served with a thick, sweet and spicy sauce that you often see at food stalls in Taiwan. You can use any kind of firm white fish for this such as cod, red snapper or Spanish mackerel.

SERVES 2
PREP TIME: 15 MINUTES
COOKING TIME: 20 MINUTES

10 oz (330 g) boneless, skinless white fish fillets

Salt, as needed

4 tablespoons potato starch or corn-starch, divided

Oil for frying

½ white onion

½ carrot

1 teaspoon sesame oil, divided

1 clove garlic, peeled and minced

A
1½ tablespoons ketchup
1 tablespoon Shaoxing wine (or sake)
2 teaspoons soy sauce
Scant ½ cup (100 ml) water
½ fresh red chili pepper (de-seeded and finely chopped)

1 tablespoon water

DIRECTIONS

1 Sprinkle the fish with salt and leave for 10 minutes. Pat dry with paper towels and cut into bite-size pieces. Dust with 2 tablespoons of the potato starch or cornstarch. Fill a pan with about ¾ inch (2 cm) of oil. Heat the oil to 340°F (170°C). Deep-fry the fish for about 4 minutes until golden brown. Take out, drain and arrange on a serving plate.

2 Thinly slice the onion lengthwise. Finely shred the carrot.

3 Heat ½ teaspoon of sesame oil and the garlic in a pan over medium heat. When the oil becomes fragrant, add the ingredients from Step **2** and stir-fry briefly. Combine the ingredients from **A** and add them to the pan. Bring to a boil while skimming off any scum.

4 Mix the water and the remaining 2 tablespoons of the potato starch or cornstarch together, and stir into the pan to thicken the sauce. Bring to a boil over high heat while adding the remaining ½ teaspoon of the sesame oil. Pour the sauce over the fish and serve.

Glass Noodle Salad with Crispy Shrimp Rolls

The distinct flavors and textures of the glass noodles, fried shrimp rolls, fresh herbs and pickled daikon radish are all tied together by the dressing. It is unforgettably delicious!

SERVES 2
PREP TIME: 30 MINUTES
COOKING TIME: 15 MINUTES

3 oz (75 g) glass or cellophane noodles

3 tablespoons Vietnamese Nuoc Mam Dressing (see page 15), divided

1 slice lemon

8 large shrimp (such as black tiger shrimp)

2 tablespoons potato starch or cornstarch

4 green onions (scallions)

8 rice paper wrappers

Sesame oil for frying

A
- 4 loose leaf lettuce leaves (torn into bite-size pieces)
- 12 leaves Thai or holy basil
- 2 teaspoons unsalted chopped peanuts
- Pickled Daikon Radish and Carrot Salad (see page 22), to taste

DIRECTIONS

1 Bring a large pan of water to a boil, add the noodles, and shut off the heat. Soak the noodles for 10 minutes until soft. Drain well, and pat dry with paper towels. Sprinkle with 1 tablespoon of the dressing, including a lemon slice (see photo a).

2 De-vein and peel the shrimp, leaving the tails. Sprinkle with the potato starch or cornstarch, and rub it in well. Rinse the starch off while rubbing the shrimp (this cleans them), and pat dry with paper towels. Make shallow incisions with a knife crosswise on the belly side of the shrimp (see photo b) to straighten them.

3 Slice the green onions into thin strips lengthwise, and then cut them into 4-inch (10-cm) pieces.

4 Put a rice paper wrapper on a piece of wax paper, and spray the surface with water until it becomes soft and pliable. Place a shrimp on top of the wrapper so that the tail sticks out from the right side. Put 4 or 5 pieces of green onion from Step **3** on top. Wrap the wrapper around the shrimp and green onions from the near side once (see photo c), and fold in the left side of the wrapper. Finish rolling up the wrapper. Repeat with all the wrappers.

5 Fill a frying pan with ¾ inch (2 cm) of sesame oil and heat it to 340°F (170°C). Add the shrimp rolls a few at a time, and fry for about 3 minutes until crispy and cooked through, turning occasionally.

6 Put the glass noodles from Step **1** on a serving plate with the ingredients in **A** and the shrimp rolls. Sprinkle with the remaining green onions, and pour on the remaining 2 tablespoons of the dressing.

It's best to mix this salad, which has so many ingredients, very well so that the dressing permeates everything before eating.

a

b

c

TIP I will never forget the first time I had *bo bun*, a soupless glass noodle dish with lots of toppings such as fried spring rolls, at a Vietnamese restaurant. I couldn't get those delicious flavors out of my mind, so I arranged them into a salad. The key to this dish is to let the dressing thoroughly permeate the softened noodles. Don't forget to add the peanuts, which provide a great crunchy accent.

Pea Shoot Salad with Shrimp and Ginger Spring Rolls

Pea shoots have a slightly grassy smell, but they are delicious eaten raw. Here I've combined them with deep-fried spring rolls, a staple of Chinese cuisine.

SERVES 2 TO 3
PREP TIME: 30 MINUTES
COOKING TIME: 20 MINUTES

8 large shrimp (such as black tiger shrimp)

2 tablespoons potato starch or cornstarch

A
- One 6-inch (15-cm) piece leek (white part), finely chopped
- One 1-inch (2.5-cm) piece fresh ginger, peeled and minced
- ⅓ teaspoon salt
- 1 tablespoon sake

B
- 1 tablespoon flour
- 1½ tablespoons water

6 spring roll wrappers

1½ oz (45 g) pea shoots

4 green onions (scallions)

2 tablespoons Chinese Five Spice Dressing (see page 15)

Oil for deep frying

DIRECTIONS

1 De-vein and peel the shrimp. Sprinkle with the potato starch or cornstarch, and rub it in well. Rinse the starch off while rubbing the shrimp (this cleans them), and pat dry with paper towels. Roughly chop the shrimp.

2 Combine the shrimp from Step **1** and the ingredients in **A** in a bowl, and mix together well. Divide into 6 portions.

3 Mix the **B** ingredients together to form a paste. Place a spring roll wrapper diagonally with a corner facing you. Place the shrimp mixture to the front of the center of the wrapper. Fold in the nearest corner and both sides, and roll the wrapper around the filling away from you. Seal the edge with the paste. Repeat with the remaining wrappers.

4 Heat the oil to 340°F (170°C). Fry the spring rolls for about 4 minutes until they turn golden brown, turning them occasionally. Once they have cooled down a little, cut each roll into three pieces.

5 Cut the green onion and pea sprouts into 1½ inch (4 cm) long pieces. Mix them with the spring rolls pieces. Add the dressing just before serving.

TIP *These simple fried spring rolls highlight the flavor of the shrimp. They go together very well with the strong flavors of the pea shoots and green onions.*

Lemongrass Meatballs with Lettuce and Shiso

This may look like a rather substantial dish, but it actually tastes very fresh and light. The refreshing flavor of lemongrass fills your mouth when you bite into one of these delicious meatballs.

SERVES 2 TO 3
PREP TIME: 20 MINUTES
COOKING TIME: 15 MINUTES

10 oz (330 g) ground pork

A
- **½ white onion, minced**
- **One 8-inch (20-cm) stalk lemongrass, minced**
- **1 fresh green chili pepper, de-seeded and minced**
- **1 clove garlic, peeled and minced**
- **½ beaten egg**
- **1 tablespoon sake**
- **1 tablespoon *nam pla***

Olive oil for frying
4 loose leaf lettuce leaves
5 green shiso leaves
2 tablespoons fresh lemon juice

DIRECTIONS

1 Put the ground pork and ingredients in **A** in a bowl, and mix well with your hands until the meat becomes sticky. Form the mixture into 1 to ⅓ inch (3 to 4 cm) diameter balls.
2 Fill a frying pan with ¾ inch (2 cm) of olive oil and heat to 340°F (170°C). Put in the meatballs from Step **1**, and fry for about 4 minutes until they turn golden brown, turning them occasionally.
3 Roughly chop the lettuce and shiso leaves.
4 Combine the meatballs, lettuce and shiso leaves in a bowl. Add the lemon juice and toss.

....

TIP Lemongrass is used frequently in Thai cuisine to add fragrance. This dish is inspired by one that I had in Thailand, where ground meat was wrapped around lemongrass stalks and grilled. The meatballs are already well seasoned with chopped lemongrass and *nam pla*, so all this dish needs is lots of lettuce and green shiso leaves, and some lemon juice to bring it all together.

Fried Bell Pepper Salad with Lemongrass Dressing

The sweetness of the deep-fried bell peppers is enhanced by the fresh lemongrass-scented dressing.

SERVES 2 TO 3
PREP TIME: 10 MINUTES
COOKING TIME: 5 MINUTES

4 small red bell peppers
4 small green bell peppers
5 fresh coriander stalks
One 8-inch (20-cm) piece lemongrass
 stalk (root end), finely chopped

A
⌈ **⅓ fresh red chili pepper, thinly**
  sliced
  3 tablespoons Thai Nam Pla Dress-
  ing (see page 15)
⌊

Oil for deep frying

DIRECTIONS

1 Poke each bell pepper 2 to 3 times with the tip of a knife. Roughly chop the coriander.

2 Soak the chopped lemongrass in water for about 3 minutes, then drain well. Combine with the dressing ingredients from **A** in a bowl.

3 Fill a pan with about ¾ inch (2 cm) of oil. Heat the oil to 355°F (180°C). Deep-fry the bell peppers for about 1 minute until just cooked through, turning occasionally.

4 Arrange on a plate, pour on the dressing, and sprinkle with the coriander.

Fried Eggplant in Ginger and Black Vinegar Dressing

Deep-frying eggplants turns them meltingly soft and sweet. The tender eggplant absorbs the richly flavored ginger dressing, creating a heavenly taste.

SERVES 2 TO 3
PREP TIME: 10 MINUTES
COOKING TIME: 10 MINUTES

6 small Japanese eggplants or 4 thin
   Chinese eggplants

A
- One 2-inch (5-cm) piece fresh ginger, peeled and shredded
- 1 tablespoon roasted white sesame seeds
- 2 tablespoons Shaoxing wine (or sake)
- 2 tablespoons black vinegar
- 2 tablespoons soy sauce

Oil for deep frying

DIRECTIONS

1 Slice the eggplants lengthwise into quarters. Soak in water for 3 minutes, drain well and pat dry with paper towels.

2 Combine the dressing ingredients in **A** in a small saucepan, and bring to a boil over medium heat. Transfer the contents to a shallow tray or bowl.

3 Heat the frying oil to 340°F (170°C). Fry the eggplants until they are tender, about 4 minutes. Put them in the dressing while they are still hot.

TIP Deep-fried eggplants appear often in Chinese cuisine, since eggplants lend themselves so well to being cooked in oil. I have fried the eggplant until they are soft and tender, and served them in a rich ginger dressing that contains Shaoxing wine and black vinegar.

Fried Green Beans with Five Spice Dressing

The five-spice-and-star-anise-scented black vinegar dressing makes me feel as if I'm back in Taiwan.

SERVES 2
PREP TIME: 5 MINUTES
COOKING TIME: 5 MINUTES

15 green beans
Oil for deep frying
4 tablespoons Chinese Five Spice Dressing (see page 15)

DIRECTIONS

1 Cut off the ends of the green beans.
2 Fill a pan with about ¾ inch (2 cm) of oil. Heat the oil to 340°F (170°C). Fry the green beans for around 2½ minutes, turning them occasionally. Arrange the green beans on a plate and pour the dressing over them while they are still hot.

Fried Scallops, Kabocha Squash and Green Onions Jeon

This dish is easy to make, looks attractive and is delicious served hot or cold. You can serve it to guests, or pack it for lunch.

SERVES 2
PREP TIME: 15 MINUTES
COOKING TIME: 20 MINUTES

5 green onions (scallions)

10 oz (330 g) kabocha squash (or substitute another sweet winter squash such as butternut squash)

8 large scallops

½ cup (60 g) cake flour

2 tablespoons sesame oil

2 eggs, beaten

A | 1 tablespoon black vinegar
   | 1 tablespoon soy sauce
   | 1 teaspoon coarsely ground red chili pepper

DIRECTIONS

1 Cut the green onions into 3 inch (8 cm) long pieces. Remove the seeds from the squash. Slice the squash into 3 inch (8 cm) long and ⅓ inch (1 cm) wide pieces.

2 Dust the scallops, green onions and squash with the flour.

3 Heat the sesame oil in a frying pan over medium heat. Dip the squash (one piece at a time), the scallops (in pairs), and the green onion (in bundles of 7 to 8 pieces) into the beaten egg. Add each piece or bundle to the pan and fry them in the oil 2 or 3 at a time.

4 When the pieces turn golden brown, flip them over, turn the heat down to low, and fry for another 3 minutes until the squash is tender. Repeat until everything is fried. Arrange all the fried pieces on a plate. Combine the **A** dressing ingredients and drizzle it over the fried pieces.

TIP *Jeon is a classic Korean dish in which vegetables, meat or seafood are dusted with flour, dipped in egg and fried. In South Korea it's often served on festive occasions like New Years.*

Chapter 6
Stir-fried Salads and Vegetables

To me, stir-fries, which are quintessentially Asian, are akin to salads since they are often packed with vegetables. In this section you'll find recipes that use the spices and seasonings from various cuisines to quickly put together a delicious, healthy dish. Not only are they great as part of a meal with plain rice, they are also great for nibbling on with your drinks!

Pork, Kimchi and Leek Salad

(photo on facing page)

This salad is built around the classic Korean combination of kimchi and pork. The *mitsuba* added at the end give this salad a refreshing taste.

SERVES 2
PREP TIME: 10 MINUTES
COOKING TIME: 10 MINUTES

5 oz (150 g) lean pork (from the leg), thinly sliced
4 oz (100 g) napa cabbage kimchi
½ leek (the white part)
¾ oz (20 g) *mitsuba* (also called Japanese parsley)

A
   2 teaspoons sesame oil
   1½ tablespoons Korean Gochujang Dressing (see page 15)
   1 tablespoon sake

DIRECTIONS

1 Cut the pork into 2-inch (5-cm) pieces. Roughly chop the kimchi. Cut the leek into thin diagonal slices. Roughly chop the *mitsuba*.
2 Heat the sesame oil in a frying pan over medium heat, and stir-fry the pork. When it starts to change color, add the kimchi and leek and stir fry-well, making sure everything is well mixed.
3 Add the ingredients in **A** and stir-fry until there is no liquid left in the pan. Turn off the heat and mix in the *mitsuba*.

Quick Stir-fry with Pea Shoots and Fried Tofu

This quick-and-easy stir-fry makes the most of the Chinese Five-Spice Dressing. Steam the pea shoots at the very end to preserve their unique flavor and texture.

SERVES 2
PREP TIME: 10 MINUTES
COOKING TIME: 10 MINUTES

4 oz (100 g) pea shoots
2 pieces (approx. 8 oz / 250 g) thick deep-fried tofu (called *atsuage*; available at Asian grocery stores—not the same as thin fried tofu or *aburaage*)
⅓ leek (the white part)
2 fresh shiitake mushrooms
1 teaspoon sesame oil
2 tablespoons Chinese Five Spice Dressing (see page 15)
1 tablespoon roasted white sesame seeds

DIRECTIONS

1 Cut the root ends off the pea shoots.
2 Cut the fried tofu into ¾-inch (2-cm) cubes. Cut the leek into ¾ inch (2 cm) long pieces. Cut the stems off the shiitake mushrooms, and quarter the caps.
3 Heat the sesame oil in a pan over medium heat. Add the ingredients from Step **2** and stir-fry until everything is lightly browned.
4 Put in the pea shoots and swirl in the dressing. Cover the pan with a lid and steam-cook for about a minute. Arrange on a serving plate and sprinkle with sesame seeds.

Sweet & Salty Pork and Water Spinach Stir-fry

This dish highlights the crisp, crunchy texture of water spinach, a vegetable that works really well in stir-fries. Because the pork is cooked until it's crispy and the fat is rendered out, it tastes quite light despite being very well flavored.

SERVES 2
PREP TIME: 10 MINUTES
COOKING TIME: 15 MINUTES

7 oz (200 g) thinly sliced pork shoulder

1 bunch water spinach (about 7 oz / 200 g—also called *kangkong*, Chinese water spinach or *kushinsai*; or substitute Swiss chard)

½ teaspoon sesame oil

A
- 1 clove garlic, peeled and crushed
- 1 tablespoon *tianmianjiang* (a sweet-salty fermented bean and wheat paste from Szechuan province in China; available at Asian grocery stores)
- 1 tablespoon Shaoxing wine (or sake)
- 1 teaspoon soy sauce

DIRECTIONS

1. Cut the pork into 1-inch (3-cm) pieces. Cut the water spinach into 2¾ inch (7 cm) long pieces. Soak the water spinach in a bowl of cold water (see photo a).

2. Heat the sesame oil and garlic in a frying pan over medium heat. When the oil is fragrant, add the pork and pan-fry it until it is crispy, diligently wiping out the excess fat and moisture from the pan with paper towels (see photo b). This is the key to making the pork crispy.

3. Combine the ingredients in **A** and add them to the frying pan. Drain the water spinach well and add it to the frying pan (see photo c). Stir-fry briefly. Serve immediately.

Be sure to eat this delicious stir-fried dish while it's still piping hot and the well-flavored pork is still crispy! It's great served with plain rice.

a

b

c

TIP Water spinach is a very popular vegetable in many Asian countries, from China to Thailand and Vietnam, and it's increasingly popular in Japan too. Here I have used it in a typically Chinese stir-fry, flavoring it with *tianmianjiang*, a salty-sweet bean and wheat paste that is popular in northern Chinese cuisine. Keep the water spinach soaking in a bowl of water until it's added to the stir-fry to retain its crispy, crunchy texture. And don't forget to frequently wipe out the excess fat in the frying pan as you cook the pork, to ensure that it will have a crispy finish.

Stir-fried Green Asparagus and Lily Bulbs

Shaoxing wine, a rice wine from China, enhances the flavors of this simple, yet elegant stir-fry. When lily bulbs are steam-fried in this way they become meaty and so delicious. I hope you'll give them a try!

SERVES 2
PREP TIME: 15 MINUTES
COOKING TIME: 10 MINUTES

4 green asparagus stalks

1 edible lily bulb (Available at Chinese grocery stores; or substitute 4 to 5 canned or bottled water chestnuts, sliced)

1 teaspoon sesame oil

One 1-inch (2.5-cm) piece fresh ginger, peeled and thinly sliced

2 tablespoons Shaoxing wine (or sake)

Salt, to taste

DIRECTIONS

1 Peel off the tough root ends of the asparagus stalks. Cut the asparagus diagonally into 2 inch (5 cm) long pieces.

2 Separate the sections of the lily bulb by peeling them off one by one (see photo b) and rinse briefly.

3 Heat the sesame oil and ginger in a frying pan over medium heat. When the oil becomes fragrant, add the ingredients from Steps **1** and **2** and stir-fry briefly.

4 Add the Shaoxing wine and cover the pan with a lid (see photo c). Steam-fry over low heat for about 2 minutes. Season with salt, to taste.

Serve this along with small plates of Cloud Ear Mushroom and Cucumber Salad (page 37) or Dried Tofu and Seaweed Salad with Black Vinegar (page 25) to recreate a Taiwanese pub in your own home.

a

b

c

TIP Lily bulbs are eaten as a vegetable in China, Korea and Japan. In Japan they're part of the traditional New Years feast, and in China they are used in stir-fries. If you can't find fresh lily bulbs, see if your Asian grocery store has precooked vacuum-packed ones as shown in photo a. This is a very simple stir-fry where the seasonings really sing, so I definitely recommend serving Shaoxing wine with it! Try adding some shrimp to the stir-fry for even more flavor and color.

Quick & Spicy Stir-fried Greens

This fragrant and simple stir fry really lets you enjoy the strong, complex flavors of *nuoc mam*, Vietnamese fish sauce. You'll want to eat this again and again.

SERVES 2
PREP TIME: 10 MINUTES
COOKING TIME: 5 MINUTES

8 oz (250 g) green leafy vegetable of your choice such as *komatsuna*, mustard greens, bok choy, *tatsoi*, water spinach or Swiss chard
1 fresh red chili pepper
1 teaspoon sesame oil
A ⎡ 1 teaspoon *nuoc mam*
  ⎣ 1 tablespoon sake

DIRECTIONS

1 Cut the greens into 3 inch (8 cm) long pieces, and soak them in a bowl of cold water until it's time to stir-fry them. This preserves their crispness. Cut the red chili pepper in half lengthwise.

2 Heat the sesame oil in a frying pan over high heat. Add the ingredients from Step **1** and stir-fry briefly. Add the ingredients in **A**, and stir-fry rapidly to mix the flavors together.

TIP   *Japanese mustard greens, cut into large pieces, and very quickly stir-fried, replace this classic recipe's usual Chinese water spinach.*

Stir-fried Chicken with Thai Basil

A variation of the classic Thai dish *pad gra pao gai*.

SERVES 2
PREP TIME: 15 MINUTES
COOKING TIME: 10 MINUTES

8 oz (250 g) boneless chicken thighs
½ red onion
2 teaspoons olive oil
One 1-inch (2.5-cm) piece fresh ginger, peeled and sliced thinly
2 tablespoons dry white wine
1 tablespoon *nam pla*
8 Thai or holy basil leaves
1 lime wedge
Coarsely ground black pepper, to taste

DIRECTIONS

1 Optionally remove the skin from the chicken. Cut the chicken into ¾-inch (2-cm) dice.
2 Cut the red onion into ¾-inch (2-cm) dice.
3 Heat the olive oil and ginger in a frying pan over medium heat. When the oil is fragrant, put in the chicken and stir-fry until browned. Sprinkle in the white wine. Stir-fry until the chicken is cooked through.
4 Add the onion and stir-fry briefly. Drizzle in the *nam pla* and turn off the heat. Tear up the basil leaves and add them to the pan, stirring quickly. Transfer to serving plates, squeeze on the lime, and sprinkle with black pepper.

Cauliflower and Potato Sabji with Parsley

Combining the soft, sweet steamed cauliflower and potato with the parsley makes this a delicious and hearty dish.

SERVES 2

PREP TIME: 15 MINUTES

COOKING TIME: 20 MINUTES

8 oz (250 g, about ½ a head) cauliflower

2 medium potatoes

1 tablespoon olive oil

1 clove garlic, peeled and minced

½ teaspoon curry powder

A ⎡ Scant ¼ cup (50 ml) dry white wine
⎣ Scant ¼ cup (50 ml) water

B ⎡ ½ teaspoons cumin powder
⎢ ⅔ teaspoon salt
⎢ Coarsely ground black pepper, to
⎣ taste

¾ oz (20 g) parsley, minced

DIRECTIONS

1 Divide the cauliflower into florets, and cut into ¾-inch (2-cm) dice. Peel the potatoes and cut into ¾-inch (2-cm) dice.

2 Heat the olive oil and garlic in a frying pan over medium heat. When the oil becomes fragrant, add the cauliflower and potato and stir-fry briefly. Add the curry powder.

3 Add the ingredients in **A** and bring to a boil. Cover the pan with a lid, turn the heat down to low, and steam-cook for about 6 minutes.

4 Remove the lid and raise the heat to medium to evaporate the excess moisture. Add the ingredients in **B** and stir-fry briefly. Transfer to a serving plate and add the parsley.

....

TIP Sabji is a classic vegetable side dish in India. It is made by steaming a variety of vegetables such as potato, cabbage and okra with spices in a pot. The cauliflower and potato version is delicious on its own, but I added lots of chopped parsley to turn it into a salad. You can mix in any baby greens of your choice instead of parsley. You can also use it as a sandwich filling.

Vegetable-packed Stir-fried Glass Noodles   Japchae

The springy, chewy glass noodles are the star of this vegetable-packed dish, which goes so well with plain rice.

SERVES 2
PREP TIME: 20 MINUTES
COOKING TIME: 10 MINUTES

2 oz (50 g) glass or cellophane noodles made with mung beans or sweet potato (the latter is called *dangmyeon*)

½ thin burdock root

½ medium carrot

2 small red bell peppers

2 thin green onions (scallions)

1 tablespoon sesame oil

One 1-inch (2.5-cm) piece fresh ginger, peeled and sliced thinly

2 tablespoons sake

2 tablespoons mirin

2 tablespoons soy sauce

Salt, to taste

DIRECTIONS

1 If using mung bean noodles, soak them in plenty of lukewarm water for 10 minutes until they soften. If using *dangmyeon*, Bring a generous amount of water to a boil and cook the noodles for 6 to 7 minutes. Drain well.

2 Finely shred the burdock root, soak in water for 3 minutes, and drain well. Finely shred the carrot, and then slice the red bell pepper thinly, and cut the green onions diagonally into ¾-inch (2-cm) pieces.

3 Heat the sesame oil and ginger in a pan over medium heat. When the oil is fragrant, add the burdock root and stir-fry. When the burdock root is crisp-tender, add the carrot and bell pepper and continue stir-frying. Add the glass noodles from Step **1** and stir-fry to combine.

4 Combine the sake, mirin and soy sauce, and add to the pan. Stir-fry until the liquid has cooked off. Season with salt, add the green onion and stir-fry quickly before serving.

TIP Japchae is one of the most popular dishes in Korean cuisine, consisting of stir-fried vegetables, meat or seafood and glass noodles. Since it has a sweet-salty flavor, it's so easy to eat. My children love it, so I make it often at home.

Stir-fried Chicken with Bamboo Shoots and Ginger

This is my take on a stir-fried oyster dish from Taiwan. If you chop up the garlic chives finely, they will be easier to eat, and it also makes them blend better with the other ingredients.

SERVES 2
PREP TIME: 15 MINUTES
COOKING TIME: 15 MINUTES

8 oz (250 g) boneless chicken thighs

1 tablespoon potato starch or cornstarch

6 garlic chives (also called Chinese
chives)

4 oz (100 g) vacuum-packed or canned
bamboo shoots

⅓ leek (the white part)

One 1-inch (2.5-cm) piece fresh ginger,
peeled and thinly sliced

2 tablespoons Shaoxing wine (or sake)

A ⌈ 1 tablespoons oyster sauce
  ⌊ 1 teaspoon soy sauce

2 teaspoons sesame oil

DIRECTIONS

1 Optionally remove the skin from the chicken. Cut the chicken into 1½-inch (4-cm) cubes and dust with the potato or cornstarch. Cut the garlic chives into ¾-inch (1-cm) pieces.

2 Slice the bamboo shoots lengthwise into ¼ inch (5 mm) thick pieces. Thinly slice the leek on the diagonal.

3 Heat the sesame oil and ginger in a frying pan over medium heat. When the oil is fragrant add the chicken and pan-fry it, turning occasionally.

4 When the chicken is browned, add the ingredients from Step **2** and stir-fry briefly. Add the Shaoxing wine, cover the pan with a lid and steam-cook over low heat for about 3 minutes.

5 Add the ingredients from **A** and mix to evenly coat everything in the pan. Add the garlic chives and stir-fry briefly.

Stir-fried King Oyster Mushrooms with Cabbage

The delicious flavor of the king oyster mushrooms is enhanced by the rich flavor of the *nam pla* and the sweetness of honey. This is a very comforting dish.

SERVES 2
PREP TIME: 10 MINUTES
COOKING TIME: 10 MINUTE

4 king oyster or *eryngii* mushrooms

3 coriander stalks

7 oz (200 g) cabbage—about ⅙ of a head

2 teaspoons sesame oil

A
- ½ fresh red chili pepper (de-seeded and chopped)
- 1 clove garlic, peeled and minced
- One 1-inch (2.5-cm) piece fresh ginger, peeled and minced
- 1 tablespoon fresh lemon juice
- 1 tablespoon *nam pla*
- 1 teaspoon honey

DIRECTIONS

1 Cut the mushrooms in half lengthwise. Thinly slice each half.

2 Mince the coriander. Slice the cabbage.

3 Heat the sesame oil in a frying pan over medium heat. Add the mushrooms and stir-fry. When they start to wilt, combine the **A** ingredients and add them to the pan. Continue stir-frying until there is very little moisture left in the pan.

4 Turn off the heat, add the coriander and mix. Transfer to serving plates.
*This dish tastes best after being left to rest for about 30 minutes. It keeps in the refrigerator for about 2 days.

TIP This recipe was inspired by a Thai dish called *yum hed*. I marinated the mushroom in chili peppers and honey, and added Thai flavor with the chopped coriander. Other mushrooms such as *shimeji*, shiitake or portabella mushrooms would be delicious too. Serving the mushrooms with shredded cabbage makes it much more salad-like.

Grilled Eggplant and Chicken Salad

The sweet, soft grilled eggplant melts in your mouth in this delicious dish. This dish is called *yum ma kuer* or *yum ma kuer yao* in Thai.

SERVES 2
PREP TIME: 10 MINUTES
COOKING TIME: 30 MINUTES

3 long, thin Chinese eggplants
½ red onion
4 fresh coriander stalks
2 teaspoons olive oil
4 oz (100 g) ground chicken
2 tablespoons Thai Nam Pla Dressing
   (see page 15), divided

DIRECTIONS

1 Poke several holes in the eggplants with a skewer or fork. Place on a grill or a grill pan over medium-low heat, and grill while rolling them around occasionally until the surfaces of the eggplants are charred. Alternatively, roast the eggplants in a 400°F (200°C) oven until softened, about 25 to 30 minutes. Turn once midway through.

2 Place the hot eggplants in a bowl of cold water, and rapidly peel off the skin. Place on paper towels to drain, and cut into bite-size pieces.

3 Thinly slice the red onion lengthwise and put into a bowl of cold water for about 3 minutes. Drain well. Roughly chop the coriander.

4 Heat the olive oil in a frying pan over medium heat and brown the ground chicken. Add 1 tablespoon of the dressing and stir-fry until there is very little moisture left in the pan.

5 Combine the ingredients from Steps **2**, **3** and **4** in a bowl, add the remaining 1 tablespoon of the dressing and toss to combine.

Fried Tofu and Bean Sprout Stir-fry

This delicious vegetarian stir-fry is called *pad tua ngok* in Thai. Although plain tofu is the norm, I have given it a twist here by using hearty, thick deep-fried tofu (*atsuage*) instead.

SERVES 2
PREP TIME: 20 MINUTES
COOKING TIME: 10 MINUTES

1 piece (approx. 4½ oz / 125 g) thick deep-fried tofu (called *atsuage*; available at Asian grocery stores)

2 small red bell peppers

2 dried wood ear mushrooms (optional)

4 oz (100 g) soy bean sprouts

1 tablespoon sesame oil

1 clove garlic, peeled and thinly sliced

A ⌐ 2 tablespoons sake
  │ 1 tablespoon *nam pla*
  ∟ 1 teaspoon honey

2 tablespoons whole unsalted peanuts

DIRECTIONS

1 Cut the thick fried tofu in half lengthwise, and slice crosswise into ⅔ inch (1.5 cm) wide pieces. Slice the bell peppers thinly lengthwise. Soak the wood ear mushrooms (if using) in lukewarm water for 15 minutes until they are softened, and cut off the stems. Shred thinly.

2 Remove the thin roots from the bean sprouts.

3 Heat the sesame oil and garlic in a frying pan over medium heat. When the oil is fragrant, add the ingredients from Step **1** and stir-fry until the tofu is browned. Add the **A** ingredients and continue stir-frying until there is very little moisture left in the pan.

4 Turn up the heat to high, add the ingredients from Step **2** and the peanuts, and stir-fry briefly.

Stir-fried Broccolini with Ginger

This simple Chinese-style stir-fry highlights the flavor and texture of broccolini, a tender cousin of broccoli.

SERVES 2
PREP TIME: 10 MINUTES
COOKING TIME: 5 MINUTES

8 broccolini stalks

2 teaspoons sesame oil

One 1-inch (2.5-cm) piece fresh ginger, peeled and thinly sliced

A ⸢ **2 tablespoons Shaoxing wine (or sake)**
⸤ **¼ teaspoons salt**

DIRECTIONS

1 Cut off the tough root ends of the broccolini stems.
2 Heat the sesame oil and ginger in a frying pan over medium heat. When the oil becomes fragrant, add the broccolini and stir-fry briefly.
3 Add the **A** ingredients to the frying pan. Cover with a lid and steam-fry for about 90 seconds.

Stir-fried Tatsoi with Black Bean Sauce

Salty, flavor-packed *douchi* or fermented black soy beans (see page 6) really bring out the flavor of the vegetables in this simple stir-fry.

SERVES 2
PREP TIME: 10 MINUTES
COOKING TIME: 5 MINUTES

3½ oz (100 g) *tatsoi* (about half a head—or substitute bok choy, *pak choi* or Swiss chard)

1 tablespoon sesame oil

1 clove garlic, peeled and roughly chopped

One 1-inch (2.5-cm) piece ginger, peeled and roughly chopped

1½ tablespoon *douchi* (Chinese fermented black soybeans)

2 tablespoons Shaoxing wine (or sake)

DIRECTIONS

1 Cut off the root end of the *tatsoi* and pull the leaves apart.
2 Bring a pan of water to a boil, add 1 teaspoon sesame oil and boil the *tatsoi* for 1 minute. Drain well and arrange on a serving plate.
3 Heat the remaining 2 teaspoons of the sesame oil, garlic, and ginger in a small pan over medium heat. Add the *douchi* and Shaoxing wine when the oil is fragrant and bring to a boil. Pour over the *tatsoi* while still hot.